the

NEW
"I DO"

RESHAPING MARRIAGE
FOR SKEPTICS,
REALISTS, AND REBELS

SUSAN PEASE GADOUA *and* VICKI LARSON

SEAL PRESS

The New "I Do"
Copyright © 2014 Susan Pease Gadoua and Vicki Larson

SEAL PRESS
A Member of the Perseus Books Group
1700 Fourth Street
Berkeley, California 94710

Library of Congress Cataloging-in-Publication Data

Gadoua, Susan Pease.
The new I do : reshaping marriage for romantics, realists, and rebels / Susan Pease Gadoua and Vicki Larson.
pages cm
ISBN 978-1-58005-545-1 (paperback)
1. Marriage. 2. Married people. 3. Man-woman relationships. 4. Interpersonal relations. 5. Marital quality. I. Larson, Vicki, 1956- II. Title.
HQ734.G1355 2014
306.81—dc23
2014009869

Cover design Erin Seaward-Hiatt
Interior design by Domini Dragoone

Distributed by Publishers Group West

To my parents, Charles and Louise, and my stepmother,
Marilyn, who sparked my initial interest in marriage, divorce,
and the inner workings of relationships.
—SUSAN

To Nash and Kit, whom I'd want to hang with even if they
weren't my children; to my late mother Trude, a marital rebel,
and my late father Bernard, who was never without a poem,
anecdote or joke; and to my journalism professor Alan Prince,
who lit a fire in me that has lasted for decades.
—VICKI

CONTENTS

INTRODUCTION

OUR MARRIAGES (AND NEAR MISSES)

Susan loved her boyfriend, whom she'd met in college, and her sparkling new engagement ring. Twenty-two years old and newly graduated, she was on the proper trajectory: get married, buy a house, and start having kids.

However, with the family dress—a gorgeous floor-length satin gown worn by three generations on her mother's side—hanging in her closet and ready to be fitted, and *Emily Post's Wedding Etiquette* on her nightstand, Susan was having doubts. Her parents had recently divorced, the final straw coming on their twenty-eighth wedding anniversary: how romantic! Unfortunately, her parents' relationship had modeled for her that marriage was a life sentence to be endured, not the happily-ever-after fairy tale she thought it should be. In the midst of picking out invitations and a reception hall, Susan got cold feet. She wasn't sure she was ready for marriage, and, despite her fiancé's disappointment, confusion, and sadness, she called off the engagement.

Vicki did not. She had just said, "I do," when she fainted, perhaps a sign of what was to come.

It wasn't how she pictured her wedding ceremony to be—flat on her back, in her beaded and feathered faux-suede wedding dress and scuffed Frye cowboy boots, cushioned by a thick, fragrant pine-needle bed on a Rocky Mountain trail with her new husband, sporting a top hat and overalls she'd embroidered with daisies, and about twelve friends (Vicki and her husband hadn't even invited their parents) staring down at her and asking, "Are you okay?"

She thought she was okay, despite the fact that, at just twenty years old, she had married her boyfriend of two years. She had somewhat foolishly dropped out of college to follow him to Colorado and tied the knot for one reason—they were in love.

Never mind that they hadn't talked about whether they wanted kids and how many, or where they were going to live, or how they were going to support themselves, or what their life goals were.

Love was enough, right?

Well, wrong. Three years later, they divorced.

While Susan's and Vicki's marriage stories are radically different—in part because Susan was wise enough to realize that love was not enough and she wasn't really marriage material yet—there is one thing they both had in common: they were guided by what family, friends, and society expected of them, and what they themselves expected.

Marriage was just what people did. But that was decades ago. Surely with so many options nowadays—from cohabitation to choice parenthood to the brave souls who blend families to the rising numbers of those who celebrate solo living—that no longer holds true.

Except in many ways, it does.

When we asked an engaged couple in their twenties why they were getting married after almost three years of living together, they responded, "It's what *normal* people do."

Susan, by that account, wasn't normal. Choosing to wait until her forties to marry for the first time, she was subjected to comments by friends, family, neighbors, and coworkers who repeatedly asked what was *wrong* with her. It was not considered natural to stay single for so long. Well-meaning people unwittingly tried to persuade Susan that she needed to find a husband rather than remain alone.

Of course, Vicki wasn't quite normal by that definition either: She married and divorced not once, but twice. She met her second husband at age twenty-nine (he was thirty-six and was also divorced), married him at age thirty-one, and had their first baby at age thirty-four. This marriage was about having kids; otherwise, they would have continued to live their rather carefree life together in their Victorian flat in a trendy San Francisco neighborhood. When they divorced after fourteen years, their boys were young, nine and twelve, but they successfully co-parented them into fine young men. While no one has told her that something must be wrong with her, you can bet they think it. Most likely, they think her marriage was a "failed marriage" because it didn't last forever. (Oddly, none of her friends gives her first marriage much credence, if any—"That marriage didn't count," they tell her.) Actually, Vicki believes her second marriage was a success; it gave them what they both wanted—children.

HOW THIS BOOK CAME TO BE

As a child of divorced parents, Susan knows firsthand how disruptive an unhappy marriage and subsequent divorce can be. When her parents split in 1981, emotional divorce support was virtually nonexistent. That experience, combined with years of working with couples in distress—whether striving to save their marriage or transition out of it—led Susan, as a licensed therapist, to channel her passion into offering support to people at perhaps one of the most crucial junctures in their lives.

What she found so striking was this: people felt incredible shame if they did not fit the marital mold. Practically everyone whose marriage ended said he or she felt like a failure or described the dissolution as a "failed marriage." But admitting something isn't working does not equal failure. In fact, it often takes more courage to go separate ways than it does to stay and pretend to the world that everything is fine.

Sadly, too many of us still think that way. If a marriage ends in divorce, people are all too eager to start pointing fingers at what went wrong—either the couple didn't understand what commitment means, or they didn't work hard enough on their marriage, or they were too focused on their own happiness, or they were too selfish or lazy.

It's still all about blame, shame, and personal failure, instead of looking at the institution of marriage itself and asking, "Why isn't it working well for about half of those who enter into it?" Actually, it isn't working well for more people than that; many couples remain married in name only because the wife or husband needs the health benefits, or they own a business and it would lead to financial ruin, or they can't afford to sell the house, or they live separate lives but decide to stick it out, unhappily, "for the kids."

While Vicki's parents may or may not have stayed married for the kids, they bickered so much that she often thought they would have been much happier if they divorced. At one point, her mother did move out of the house—actually, she moved to another state for about ten years. At the time, Vicki—in her self-absorbed twenties and newly married to her first husband—didn't realize that her mother, then in her early forties, was somewhat of a rebel. It took guts for a middle-aged woman to up and leave her comfortable suburban New York City home and buy a condo in Miami—a city where she knew no one but a daughter, Vicki's older sister—get a job, and start a new life for herself, albeit with her husband joining her once a month for a long weekend. It wasn't until Vicki was in her late forties and twice divorced that she sat her mom down and asked her, "What was *that* all about?"

"I'd had enough," was all her mother said. With many years of marriage behind her, Vicki knew what her mother meant. Eventually, her father permanently joined her mom in Florida, and they lived together in somewhat peaceful coexistence until they passed away after sixty-one years of marriage.

There are many other people like Vicki's mother, people who are willing to change what clearly isn't working. Couples are tweaking the institution to fit their needs even if it looks pretty much like a traditional marriage from the outside. Serial monogamy, blended families, open marriages, covenant marriages, commuter marriages—these variations-on-a-theme arrangements are already happening. We wrote *The New I Do* because we believe it's time to end the blaming, shaming, and sense of failure many feel, as well as the notion that some people need to keep their marital choices in the closet lest they be judged.

We hope to change that. We hope to normalize what is already happening. And, just as important, we want to offer those who may want to marry one day—perhaps even you—or those who would like to transform their marriage, a few new marital road maps that will set them up for success. We know it won't be easy. We're asking you to let go of the vision you have in your head of what marriage "looks like." Amazingly enough, a 1950s model of family persists today even though so few of us live in those sorts of families, even though we have so many more options than men and women had back then, as sociologist Stephanie Coontz has so exhaustively detailed in her books, including *Marriage, a History* and *The Way We Never Were*. We thank Coontz and other researchers who have been willing to put marriage under a microscope. We also thank those of you who not only have paid attention to the shifts in the institution of marriage but who also are willing to explore ways to make it work better for more people and who have shared your thoughts and stories with us. We have changed your names in this book, but your stories are honest and real.

A DO-IT-YOURSELF MARRIAGE

If you picked up this book, you most likely are entertaining the idea of getting married, if not immediately, then one day. Or, you are in a stagnant long-term marriage and you're looking for creative ways to reinvent your relationship in the hopes of avoiding divorce. You probably know that there is no shortage of books on the subject, shelved as marriage-advice books. Maybe you've flipped through the pages on marriage tips, skimmed a chapter or two, or read an excerpt in a magazine. Even if you haven't, you can guess what's inside. The "secrets" those books will no doubt cover are how to improve communication, resolve conflict, manage expectations, and enhance intimacy and sex.

While we don't have anything against books that help people discover or rediscover ideas to boost romance or communication, *this is not one of those books*. This is not a how-to guide to help you keep your marriage alive or exciting. And it most definitely is not a manual that offers secrets of living "happily ever after."

This is a book about redefining marriage—*your* marriage, and marriage in general.

Our hope is that you will think more consciously about what kind of marriage suits you. It may look nothing like the union your parents, relatives, friends, or—heaven forbid—celebrities have. We want to challenge you to ask yourself what you truly want and need from a marriage and help you find a way to express this to your partner with honesty and clarity.

Whether you are thinking about getting married for the first and only time or if you are wondering if you should say "I do" for the second, third, fourth, or tenth time, or if you are curious about re-creating the marriage you are in, we will offer you different ways to be a couple so that whichever model you choose, you will be more likely to succeed.

If, like us, you have seen marriages around you end in separation and divorce, this book is for you. If you have seen marriages remain intact even if they're unhappy, sex-deprived, and loveless, this book is for you. If you are questioning whether marriage is still worth it, this book is most definitely for you. And, if you're in a marital rut, this book is for you. Couples often run to therapists or self-help books to "work" on a troubled marriage, whether to boost their communication or intimacy or to lessen their conflict. Again, those skills are nice in concept, but they don't always work. We believe couples might want to consider renegotiating the terms of their marital contract to better fit their needs and goals as their life circumstances change.

Most couples enter marriage believing they will do things differently; they'll be better, smarter, more intuitive, and more in tune than everyone else. But as long as they keep entering into the same marital model—traditional marriage—their good intentions will often reach the same results. We should mention that we believe in marriage. We are rooting for marriage. But we recognize that the marital model in our modern-day culture sets up too many people for failure.

"We have unprecedented latitude to define marriage in our own image, and not in our parents' image," notes Pamela Haag in her book *Marriage Confidential: The Post-Romantic Age of Workhorse Wives, Royal Children, Undersexed Spouses, and Rebel Couples Who Are Rewriting the Rules*. The real opportunity and potential of her marriage generation, she laments, is not being taken advantage of because marriage hasn't been redefined.

Until now, that is.

Chapter One

HAVE WE OUTGROWN MARRIAGE?

———————————————•———————————————

"Marriage is neither heaven nor hell, it is simply purgatory."
—Abraham Lincoln

*M*arriage as we know it is dying.

Don't just take our word for it—look at what's happening around you: More than ever before, people are living together without tying the knot, more men and women are delaying marriage or opting out altogether, more couples are having babies outside of marriage, and about half of all marriages still end in divorce. Today, "it is possible to live, love, form a family without sex, without children, without a shared home, without a partner, without a working husband, without a heterosexual orientation, or without a 'biological' sexual body," notes sociologist Elisabetta Ruspini.

Perhaps this is an indication that the institution as we've practiced it actually needs to die.

That may be an odd statement in a book about marriage, especially a book that's *for* marriage. Yes, we are for marriage. But it's clear that couples are already creating romantic partnerships that resist the one-size-fits-all model of marriage that's been presented to them. Rather than continue to encourage people to cram themselves into an old model that isn't working for many—about one out of two marriages ends in divorce—we want to acknowledge what's already happening and encourage you to think about new ways to marry.

Yes, we have the audacity to ask you to throw out whatever image of marriage you have circling around in your mind and start from scratch. Forget you even have a concept of what marriage looks like, especially if it's been tainted by rom-coms, where the boy always gets the girl even though they have issues; TV shows like *The Bachelorette*, which promote the idea that true love (and a one-carat rock) can really happen in just six weeks; magazines pressuring that you answer "Why Won't He Commit?" or instructing you how to "Get Your Man to Say, 'I Do'"; and "experts" advising you on the "Five Sure-Fire Signs You've Found The One." While you're at it, please shred the marital messages you got from observing your parents' marriage, too, or your BFF's.

Instead, we are challenging you to imagine that, if you were responsible for building a new model of marriage, what would it look like? What would you do differently? What would you throw out altogether? What would you keep? What kind of marriage do *you* want?

Then we're going to help you get it.

It isn't enough to change your attitude and expectations about marriage. That has already been happening with little to no success in changing the way people actually marry. What we are calling for is basically an Occupy Marriage movement. Instead of taking part in more "until death do us part" marriages—except for those of you who consciously choose that that's what you want—we're calling for marriages that are renewable, meaning each spouse will need to be paying closer attention to his or her actions and stick to what was agreed to lest his or her partner decides not to renew a few years down the road. We're calling for marriages that recognize some people's voracious sexual desires while also wanting long-term loving and committed partnerships. We're calling for marriages that allow each partner's freedom and space while keeping the couple intimately connected and committed. We're calling for marriages where spouses are mature and secure enough to keep things together so they can provide their kids with a stable and consistent home life in order for them to thrive.

MARRIAGE TODAY: CRISIS OR OPPORTUNITY?

Across the globe, the bar keeps getting raised on what needs a spouse should meet. A wife or a husband is expected to be soul mate, lover, best friend, co-parent, great communicator, romantic, intellectual, and professional equal, companion, and financial partner, and also provide happiness, fulfillment, financial stability, intimacy, social status, fidelity . . . well, you get the idea. By the way, if you have actually met someone like that, please let us know because in all our years of dating, marrying, coupling, talking to singles and couples, and research, we have never come across anyone who was able to do that, not even well, but at all. You might want to check in with your own conscious or unconscious list of must- and must-not-haves in a partner.

"Never before in history has any culture expected so much from this union as we currently do in the Western world," writes sociologist Stephanie Coontz in *Marriage, a History.* "The adoption of these unprecedented goals for marriage [have] had unanticipated and revolutionary consequences that have since come to threaten the stability of the entire institution."

Said another way, the attempt to make marriage meet each person's many needs is a setup for failure. And fail it has. Not for everyone, but certainly for far too many. We can't think of any other social paradigm where the odds of success—defined as happily staying together forever—are so low, yet nothing is being done to improve it.

The only logical explanation for continuing to try to push traditional marriage on everyone is that society is in denial about the fact that the likelihood of lasting "until death do us part" happily is grim. Having surveyed hundreds of people about their marriages, we learned that many thought they would beat the odds, only to find that their marriage took on a different quality—a spouse decided marriage wasn't for him or her after all; a spouse changed or didn't change; an addiction developed; tragedy struck, and the couple never healed or healed differently; a spouse became attracted to another person or another gender; a spouse actually became another gender or came out as gay; the kids proved to be too much responsibility or a major source of disagreements. Regardless of the reason, game-changers happen, and even the best of intentions and fervent exchanges of vows couldn't make things work.

All that was left was a sense of being marginalized by others because they somehow "failed" at their union. Along with these types of problems that couples encountered in their marriage, ugly, messy, expensive, and often drawn-out divorces served to solidify a collective aversion to connubial coupling. Instead of reshaping marriage, many people have just stopped tying the knot formally. Here's what the numbers reveal:

More couples are opting to live together rather than trek down to city hall before witnesses to profess their commitment, although many cohabitors eventually marry or break up. Countries such as Denmark, France, and Canada have seen a spike in civil unions, which only became available in the United States in 2001, followed by domestic partnerships. Society overall has become more accepting of these alternatives to traditional marriage, but no alternative has satisfyingly replaced it. The long fight by gays and lesbians to legally marry shows just how much marriage still matters.

In addition to the declining numbers of marrying couples in the United States, more than half (53 percent) of children born to women under age thirty today are born to women who didn't get married, although many of them live with the baby's father. And in women of all ages, there has been a 600 percent increase in single motherhood since 1960.

This would have been unheard of just a few decades ago. There is a socioeconomic divide, too; college-educated couples are much more likely to tie the knot than others, as are whites. Increasingly, marriage is becoming a luxury good. With so many forms of family accepted today, there's relatively little that marriage offers that isn't available otherwise. As a result, rather than being *the* lifestyle choice for adults, tying the knot has become *one of several* lifestyle choices. For the first time in history, marriage has extremely viable competition.

All of this has been creating a lot of anxiety for a lot of people who wring their hands and see what is happening as a crisis. We prefer to see it as an opportunity. Given these huge sociological events, we believe it's time to be more creative with matrimony by legally bending the institution to meet more of society's present-day needs. Actually, we'd like to do more than just bend marriage. We want to reinvent it so it matches what people are already doing. In order to do that, society—and yes, you—needs to stop clinging to some nostalgic past.

WHAT ARE WE ACTUALLY CLINGING TO?

Marriage hasn't always looked like the way we practice it today. You might be surprised to discover that the marriage most people have—what's typically referred to as "traditional" marriage—is anything but traditional. In fact, marriage has twisted, turned, transformed, and, been reinvented many times since the concept began, and, in places like Africa or remote villages in China and India, it looks nothing like what couples in the Americas have. So, when you hear people talk about "traditional" marriage, you need to ask, *which* "traditional" marriage?

Before we can explore new ways to marry, let's step back and take a brief look at how society got into this marital mess. A good place to start is just before the 1950s, the era that defines what traditional marriage looks like for most people (although it actually started way before).

The post–World War II years brought a new appreciation for home and family, and for new technology. It's doubtful the inventors of television hoped to transform people's concept of marriage, but that's exactly what happened. Until TV came along, few people knew what other people's family life looked like; now there were shows like *Father Knows Best, Dennis the Menace,* and *Leave It to*

Beaver to model "normal" families. Except, of course, few families actually lived happily like that, then or now. Commercials also sold people idealized images of what marriage was all about—the house in the suburbs with the white picket fence, the successful male breadwinner, the happy female homemaker, and 2.5 charming and obedient children.

THE 1940S: FOR BETTER OR FOR WORSE

During the war years, women were thrust into jobs typically done by men. After the war, however, they were expected to step down from performing "men's work" and go back to being wives and mothers as they had been before. The problem was that the so-called weaker gender had proved itself to be as capable as men in the work world. This gave women a sense of empowerment and a bigger sense of purpose. When they were no longer needed in the same capacity, they were brushed aside and told they weren't being ladylike. The seeds of women's liberation and equal opportunity had been planted, and this movement, as you'll see in a minute, went on to have a major influence on marriage and divorce.

Nonetheless, many women let go of their higher aspirations and returned to the old script. Those who refused to conform to the role of housewife and mother were severely criticized. A 1947 best-selling book, *The Modern Woman*, called feminism a "deep illness," labeled the idea of an independent woman a "contradiction in terms," and reasoned that women who sought equal pay and equal educational opportunities were engaging in a "ritualistic castration of men." Sometimes wives who wanted no part of what society expected of them were labeled schizophrenic, were institutionalized, and occasionally were given shock treatments "to accept their domestic roles and their husbands' dictates."

Although marriage counseling began in the 1930s, it began to pick up steam in the 1940s as an increasing number of marital "experts" convinced World War II brides that it was their job to make a happy marriage and home, setting the stage for the growth of marriage counseling, the idea that marriage is work, and a multimillion-dollar self-help industry to help couples keep their marriage intact. And as historian Kristin Celello writes in *Making Marriage Work: A History of Marriage and Divorce in the Twentieth-Century United States*, "In the ensuing years, the ability to hold a marriage together, for better or for worse, became the very definition of marital and wifely success."

WE WILL NOT QUIETLY GO BACK TO THE 1950S

For young girls growing up in the '50s, the key to a successful life depended on how they were able to answer these three essential questions one day: Are you married, what does your husband do, and do you have any children? Girls were groomed for one thing and one thing only—domesticity.

Men didn't escape societal expectations, either. Although they were presented as "kings of their castles," they had few other options than to work hard, often at corporate jobs that were soulless. Many began to see the traditional masculine role as a trap. Masculinity was defined by conformity and self-denial. They may have been good providers, but they were often silent and distant figures to their children and emotionally disconnected from their wives.

"In the 1950s, there was a firm expectation (or, as we would say now, 'role') that required men to grow up, marry, and support their wives. To do anything else was less than grown-up, and any man who willfully deviated was judged to be somehow less than a man," writes Barbara Ehrenreich in *The Hearts of Men: American Dreams and the Flight from Commitment*.

THE 1960S: CRACKS IN THE HAPPY MARRIAGE FACADE

By the time the 1960s rolled around, the cracks in the facade of the "happy family" marital model became evident. Despite that, the model remained intact, but not unquestioned. Betty Freidan's 1963 best seller, *The Feminine Mystique*, brought into the national consciousness what many college-educated suburban mothers were

privately feeling—the "happy family" was nowhere near as fulfilling as the media presented it, but they struggled with guilt for
wanting more.

This decade also saw marriage move from being a companionate
type of relationship, which focused on the satisfaction and pleasure
that come from playing the role of spouse, to a more individualized
type of relationship, which emphasized personal fulfillment and
self-actualization.

When the birth control pill started being used commercially, it
was transformational for women. With the fear of an unwanted pregnancy behind them (for the most part), young unmarried women had
more choices than ever before about what their futures might look
like, including delaying marriage.

Communes started popping up across the United States.
Rather than one man and one woman pairing up, many communes
were designed to accommodate "free love," without the rigid para-
digms that had previously been in place, as well as a desire to create
new family units. Some women were drawn to communal living as a
way to break the isolation that comes with raising children as well
as the dependence on their husbands for adult contact. Some men
saw it as a way to free themselves from "financial insecurity and
the rat-race," and as a way to pool resources and thus beef up their
standard of living.

Marriage counselors began helping to push along the idea of
self-fulfillment and personal growth in marriage, and couples were
encouraged to communicate their feelings.

THE 1970S: PEACE, LOVE, AND FREEDOM

The 1970s, more than any other period in society's recent past, gave
way to altered social patterns that would impact marriage. New gender norms provided a turning point for the role of girls, and, in turn,
marriage. Title IX, enacted in 1972, changed forever how girls were
educated in America, which shifted their trajectory. No longer was
college the place for women to go to meet men and get a Mrs. degree;
it became a place for them to prepare for a career.

Then no-fault divorce was passed into law, which made it easier for couples to divorce. Husbands and wives no longer had to prove wrongdoing in order to dissolve their marriage. Anyone who wanted out of wedlock could get out. As a result, America saw the dissolution rate more than double, going from 20 percent to 50 percent almost overnight.

There was a third factor in the changing face of marriage. The '70s gave rise to the Me Generation. The nation saw a shift from marriage-as-obligation with relatively low expectations to one with heightened expectations. People began asking more from their spouses and from marriage itself. The idea of choosing a soul mate was introduced to couples.

The era also saw a rise of marriage enrichment programs that promoted traditional gender roles as a way to marital nirvana—no doubt as a backlash to rising divorce rates and the women's movement—while other programs focused instead on boosting communication and making marriage a partnership.

Although divorce wasn't yet depicted in the '70s prime-time TV shows, *The Brady Bunch* was the first to portray a blended family of his three boys and her three girls (according to the storyline, parents Carol and Mike were both widowed before meeting—much more palatable than being divorced).

Perhaps the biggest marital shakeup was the beginning of the push for the right to marry by gays and lesbians. In 1970, Jack Baker and Michael McConnell from Hennepin County, Minnesota, applied for a marriage license. They were the first gay couple to ever attempt this. The application was flat-out rejected. Baker, a law student, predicted that some day, gay men would legally be able to marry. He did some advocacy work for the cause and even ran for public office, but lost.

While the Pill continued to be widely used for preventing pregnancy, the sexual revolution saw the introduction of many more sexually transmitted diseases. Also during this time, scientists in England were experimenting with ways to help those who wanted children but couldn't get pregnant. In 1978, the world welcomed its first test-tube baby, Louise Brown.

THE 1980S: THE ERA OF DIVORCE

After decades of rising numbers of couples tying the knot, 1980 marked a turning point in the increase of never-marrieds. By 1985, the United States saw the average age of first marriages begin to rise across gender and culture lines, blacks and whites, males and females. This was the beginning of the upward trend in age of first-time marriers that is still in play today.

More women worked outside the home, but what was most remarkable was that women's careers were becoming less subordinate to men's; from the late 1970s through the '90s, the number of women who were managers more than doubled.

The most notable trend for marriage during the 1980s was the un-marrying; the divorce rate grew 200 percent from what it had been in the 1960s. The values that had once been placed so high on marriage were disintegrating: waiting until after being legally married to lose one's virginity was no longer necessary (perhaps more applicable to females than males), and societal pressure to marry if a couple became pregnant was waning (when was the last time you heard of someone having a "shotgun wedding"?). Despite all the good news, a cover story in *Newsweek* magazine indicating that college-educated women who were still single at age forty were more likely to be killed by a terrorist than they were to find a husband created angst for legions of women that lasted decades and permeated pop culture. (The magazine retracted the story in 2006, but the idea of the "terminally single woman" remained stuck in the minds of many women for years.)

Despite traditionalists' fighting to maintain the status quo, the '80s were a time of tremendous change and of breaking out of outdated and often stuffy cultural norms. This was made apparent by the changes in the media. Madonna's suggestive lyrics on her 1984 hit "Like a Virgin" as well as her flamboyant sexuality on stage were like nothing seen before (although it seems mild in comparison to many of the songs and singers today). Television shows like *Married . . . with Children* and *The Cosby Show* portrayed much more realistic versions of marriage and family life than in decades past.

In the 1980s, scandals, sex, and violence were prevalent in all forms of media, and advertising glorified the kind of wealth, beauty, and success few could achieve. With the growth of personal computers, the Internet brought seemingly endless reams of information that stimulated, excited, and overwhelmed. "More" became an American buzzword.

The fight for marriage for same-sex couples was all but dormant until the late 1980s, when the AIDS epidemic that ravaged gay communities across the country made many start to be aware of the inequality concerning inheritance and death benefits. In May 1989, Denmark established registered partnerships that granted same-sex couples many of the rights associated with marriage.

As the world's first test-tube baby celebrated her third birthday, in-vitro fertilization was introduced to the United States, giving women more options than ever and allowing them to not be so focused on their biological clocks.

THE 1990S AND BEYOND

With marriage rates dropping and divorce rates on a steep ascent, people began to feel concerned about the state of marital affairs. A 1995 report by a conservative group proclaimed that marriage rates were declining because people weren't taking the institution seriously enough. It urged Americans to focus on making marriage work rather than succumb to the "divorce revolution" culture that caused countless children to suffer. Believing that the fabric of America was torn, the group urged citizens to restore the idea of lasting marriages. But the pleas fell on deaf ears. The divorce rates continued to hover at or around the 50 percent mark, where they remain today.

Not everyone snubbed marriage, however. At the same time that hetero couples were rejecting the institution, same-sex couples wanted in. Gay men and lesbians were tired of being discriminated against and began loudly demanding equal rights when it came to having their unions recognized by the government and receiving all the legal and financial perks their straight friends were getting.

In response to the "gay threat" and as a way to "preserve" marriage, the Defense of Marriage Act (DOMA) became federal law in 1996. The law established the definition of marriage as being between a man and a woman, and it gave states permission to refuse to recognize marriages between same-sex couples. It was a setback and a shock to those who had worked so hard for equality—especially since a Democratic president, Bill Clinton, signed it into law. But advocates of marriage for same-sex couples persevered. It would be another sixteen-plus years before DOMA was ruled unconstitutional in 2013. Many states have since passed laws recognizing marriage for same-sex couples, and there is increasing pressure on states that have refused to pass similar laws.

In 2004, then-President George W. Bush began a multiyear, billion-dollar campaign to promote marriage to low-income couples as their ticket out of poverty—a controversial campaign that continues today. Many would say that the campaign has failed.

WHERE WE ARE TODAY

When you think of what a typical American family looks like today, what comes to mind? Does it look like your longtime friend, a single parent of three? Your childfree interracial neighbors two houses down? The principal of your kids' school who is getting married next month for the third time and blending five children into a new home? Your gay coworker who recently tied the knot and is in the process of adopting a child? Your cousin who lives in a classic nuclear family in a Midwest suburb (with requisite picket fence, dog, and minivan)? Does it look like your own family? Is your family "normal," or are you a product of divorce, blended families, mixed races, or a single parent?

In truth, a "typical" family isn't so typical anymore. There's no one straight path to creating a family. As professor and author Andrew Cherlin says, "This churning, this turnover in our intimate partnerships is creating complex families on a scale we've not seen before. It's a mistake to think this is the endpoint of enormous change. We are still very much in the midst of it."

A LONG TIME AGO IN A CITY
(OR CASTLE OR CAVE) NEAR YOU

So, what did marriage look like before the traditional marriage model of the 1950s? Well, a lot of different things. Pair bonding goes back about two and a half million years ago to the Stone Age. Even then, people seemed to have a need for social control, stability, and accountability. Since this predates recorded history, we'll never really know just how Homo sapiens structured their mating. But, given how primitively they lived, it's safe to assume they were less interested in finding "the love of their life" and more driven by the instincts to survive and procreate.

The first recorded marriage is believed to be about 4,000 years ago in Mesopotamia. With basic needs met, life was less of a challenge for people, so unions during this time period were designed more for the purpose of keeping wealth and resources in the family and for producing heirs. The word "matrimony" is derived from the Latin word "*mater*," which means "mother." In fact, it was common for first and second cousins to marry to strengthen family ties.

Throughout Roman history, there were several variations on the marriage theme. At one point, three levels of nuptials were available—*Confarreatio*, which had a more religious overtone and the most formal ceremony; *Coemptio*, which emphasized the business aspect of unions and had a less-formal marriage ceremony; and *Usus*, a marriage that occurred by default once a couple lived together for a year, no ceremony required.

Pre-Islamic societies in the Middle East practiced a tradition called a *mut' a*, a temporary marriage granted under certain circumstances that allowed men and women to have sex without being penalized. Once the temporary marriage contract was over, the couple could go their separate ways with no further obligation. If a child was born from their union, the baby would be considered legitimate and had rights to the father's inheritance.

Ironically, the church originally was against marriage. As Elizabeth Gilbert writes so delightfully in *Committed: A Love Story*, the church regarded "monogamous marriage as marginally less wicked than flat-out whoring—but only very marginally." The church decided to get involved with marriage when it realized people were going to marry anyway, with or without its blessings. From a religious perspective, marriage got "promoted" from a civil event to a holy union, and, in 1215, it was further boosted when it was deemed one of the seven Catholic sacraments (along with baptism, confirmation, and penance). This is when "until death do us part," became integrated into the vows.

Throughout most of history, love really had no place in marriage. Marriage was still a business deal for the purpose of gaining heirs and power. Arranged marriages were much more common and were based on what political positioning or power the partnership would bring. The concept of Prince Charming would not have entered a little girl's imagination because these arranged marriage contracts were not about saving her from singlehood (or her needs at all); rather, the unions were foisted on women as a vehicle for men to get their agendas satisfied, be they political, social, fiscal, or sexual. Indeed, marriage was often a raw deal for women.

Love not only didn't enter the picture, but it was also believed to be unacceptable or at the very least foolish to base marriage on something as changeable and volatile as love by many cultures throughout the world. In fact, the term "lovesick" was used by the Greeks to describe a form of insanity. Indeed, love in marriage was seen as ludicrous, immoral, and even detrimental, as it posed a threat to other important relationships, such as the alliance with parents or a detraction from one's devotion to God. While some couples today may put God before each other, we guess few would be more devoted to their parents than to their spouse.

Early modern Europeans even had a saying, "He who marries for love has good nights and bad days." We'd say married couples nowadays whose love has gone by the wayside are having bad days *and* bad nights. Of course, if a couple fell in love *after* they married, that was one thing, but to choose a lifelong mate based on emotions rather than suitability and purpose was a ridiculous and irresponsible notion.

Yet love persevered. Romance in marriage became socially acceptable at the end of the seventeenth and beginning of the eighteenth centuries. The Enlightenment saw the culmination of the advancement of science and discovery, and the church was no longer in charge to the degree it had been as people began to think more independently and openly. Despite the common belief that today's emphasis on happiness in a marriage is a recent requirement, the idea of pursuing a life and relationships for the sake of happiness versus for religious reasons or for social or financial gain emerged around this time. That is, thankfully, one less thing that can be blamed on Boomers, Gen-Xers, or Millennials.

Romance continued to blossom in the mid-1800s with the Victorian era, and, though it had previously been feared as a "dangerous amusement," romantic love in marriage finally prevailed over the business of marriage. The Industrial Revolution in the nineteenth century made life easier for much of the West. This meant that marriage could be more of an option than an obligation. People began to pick partners based on love—even when their parents disapproved. Divorce rates, while still low compared with today's rates, rose because people in unhappy or abusive marriages could leave.

Now society is experiencing a technological revolution that is rapidly transforming not only the way people work, play, think, and communicate with each other, but also the way people love. Some predict society is not far off from welcoming artificially intelligent humanlike robots into people's daily lives. If that happens, then it's likely there will be robot-human love and robot-human sex. Where there's sex, there's infidelity; will the next spike in divorce be over robot-human trysts?

So, where does that leave you? In a curious place when it comes to love and marriage. Love, which was long thought to be detrimental to marriage, is not just expected in a marriage nowadays, but is a requirement. "Love has indeed triumphed over marriage, but now it is destroying it from the inside," opines French writer Pascal Bruckner in his slim book *Has Marriage for Love Failed?* "Married life used to be a prison cell; now it seems to be transforming itself into a sobering-up cell. We have not found the remedy for the sufferings of love, any more than our ancestors did."

HOW DO WE GET UNSTUCK?

Like most species, humans are wired to pair up and mate. Humans are also creatures of habit. Having a formal and steady construct in which to couple makes good sense for a number of reasons, especially if you plan to have children. Yet the marital model people have held on to so dearly is faltering for many. That's because the model is still based on survival, procreation, property, and wealth. But as you've seen, the push toward marrying for love instead of marriage's historical purposes means that the marital contract needs to be updated.

Why has society been so reluctant to change? We believe out of fear. Changing what people know and feel comfortable with is scary. "We've always done it this way," many people insist. "If we allow people to marry whomever and however they want, all hell will break loose." Except it hasn't: people are already marrying "whomever and however they want."

One reason we wrote this book is to name that so society can strip away the shame, blame, and judgments that accompany coupling choices that venture outside the mainstream. Why? Most people consciously or unconsciously perpetuate beliefs that society should stick to traditions around marriage and family. If you look back at other eras and compare marriage then and now, you see that there have been as many ways to couple and marry as there have been cultures. In fact, the models we introduce to you in this book already exist—starter, Living Apart Together, open, companionship, covenant, safety, and parenting marriages. Not only that, but Western culture is just one culture among thousands around the world. You may be surprised to see what marriage looks like elsewhere.

In parts of West Africa, some women in certain circumstances can have a "female husband" so they can remain with their in-laws if widowed or be a "mother" even if they are unable to have children. Some cultures have been practicing Living Apart Together marriages long before their more-recent trendiness. Males of the Gurumba tribe of New Guinea, for example, work and sleep separately from their wives. The Na of southwestern China make raising children the primary focus of their family, so much so that the mother and father may only have sex once and never see each other again. The child is subsequently parented by not only the mother but also her brothers and sisters. The Na keep the emphasis on maintaining close blood, rather than in-law, family ties, and the tradition has been passed down for generations. This certainly raises the question of how much parents need to be in love with each other to successfully raise a child, which we address later in the book.

Open marriages and polygamy (having more than one spouse, whether a man having several wives, called *polygyny*, or a woman having several husbands, called *polyandry*) have been around as long as marriage itself. Even today, it is accepted in parts of Europe, the Middle East, and Asia to have an extramarital lover. Although in some cases it is done covertly, it is much more widely accepted than in the United States, where it is considered scandalous.

There are marriages that many might view as downright bizarre. Sri Lankans deem a couple married if the woman cooks for the man—and divorced when she stops cooking for him (how much simpler than divorcing in Western states!). The Vanatinai society near Papua, New Guinea, judges a relationship as being formalized when a couple starts eating together. Marriage for India's Toda people is negotiated when children are two or three years old and celebrated at maturity. And for some Cantonese people in China, daughters may marry a dead person.

Yet with all these variations on coupling and family, the one commonality is that a workable social order can be found in a wide range of practices. All hell has not broken loose, and people have created ways of living together that have not only stood the test of time but have also worked for their particular needs and their culture.

As we said earlier, traditional marriage is hardly traditional, and many of the marital traditions were oppressive—especially for women. We don't want to go back to that. Do you?

MARRIAGE, THE GREAT EXPERIMENT

"What is happening to 'married pairs'? They are almost extinct."

"Marriage has become difficult, and if it is not to be a barrier to
happiness, it must be conceived in a somewhat new way. . . . If
marriage is to achieve its possibilities, husbands and wives must
learn to understand that whatever the law may say, in their
private lives, they must be free."

Those laments may sound familiar, but they're hardly new; in fact,
both were written in the 1920s, an era when marriage and monogamy went under the societal microscope as they never had before.
Throughout the early 1900s, there was a deluge of writing about
marriage and divorce—from government reports to novels, plays,
and memoirs, from sociological studies to newspaper articles, all
with pretty much the same message: marriage was in desperate
need of reform. The answer for luminaries such as H. G. Wells, Bertrand Russell, Edith Wharton, and Vera Brittain was to re-create
marriage. For them, mutually satisfying sex and affection between
the sexes were more important than the blessing of a priest or jus-
tice of the peace; once that was in place, they believed, voluntary
monogamy would replace compulsory monogamy.

There were even calls to abolish marriage outright. That was
never going to happen, George Bernard Shaw knowingly wrote, but
he did predict that "the progressive modification of the marriage contract will be continued until it is no more onerous nor irrevocable
than any other commercial deed of partnership."

Despite their individual efforts to experiment with open
marriages and alternative ways of living and loving, the progressive couples of the early twentieth century never quite achieved
what they wanted, and while society is closer to Shaw's business-
contract-like version than ever before, the traditional marriage
contract still feels pretty onerous.

Thankfully, marriage today is less about shared production,

with a wife as homemaker and a husband as breadwinner, as it is about shared consumption—activities that are more enjoyable when shared with a loved one, whether a sport or participating in a community (such as attending a church, mosque, or synagogue together) or raising children in partnership. And the way couples marry nowadays reflects that.

Many young couples have changed their expectations about marriage; they want an egalitarian model in which each shares breadwinning, housekeeping, and childrearing. While that sounds good in theory, what all too often happens is that, when children come along (for those couples that want children), that's harder to accomplish, and guess what—more men expect their wives to cut back on their work hours and focus on homemaking and family. Not to say that some women don't want that, too, but the vast majority would rather work—even preferring divorce over homemaking, according to Kathleen Gerson's *The Unfinished Revolution: How a Generation Is Reshaping Family, Work, and Gender in America.* Still, that desire has paved the way for many more men to become stay-at-home dads.

So, while society has experienced a mini-rebellion of that 1950s male breadwinning model, it still is the unconscious default for far too many of us. Could couples individualize their marriage contract to better fit their needs?

We say yes.

We say they should.

We say it's time.

What if society revisited purpose-driven marriages and deemed them acceptable or, preferably, even better than love-driven marriage? Rather than expecting one person to meet all your needs, you might ask a spouse to meet a few, and you'd be encouraged to get other needs met in other ways or with other people or in some combination. Maybe you want to partner for the sole reason of having children and co-parenting, and have passion and sex outside the marriage. Maybe you prefer to partner for companionship instead of expecting a spouse to support you financially. Maybe you want to partner solely for financial security and enjoy social activities and vacations with family or friends.

As we mentioned earlier, these alternative marriages are already being practiced in our culture, but often privately, for fear of shame and judgment. We believe people have the right to marry for whatever reasons they want. We also believe that the more society honors the different choices people make, the more the institution will be strengthened—not weakened.

And that means we need to let go of the belief that marriage must be forever; it already isn't for far too many couples. Couples that want to create a marriage that lasts forever are certainly free to do that, and each person would be wise to find a like-minded partner. But the "until death do us part" model must be a free choice, not a societal expectation.

"Liberating ourselves from the traditional strictures of marriage altogether, and/or transforming those strictures to include all of us—gay, feminist, career-focused, baby crazy, monogamous, non-monogamous, skeptical, romantic, and everyone in between—is the challenge facing this generation," writes Courtney E. Martin, author of *Do It Anyway: The New Generation of Activist*. "As we consciously opt out or creatively reimagine marriage one loving couple at a time, we'll be able to shift societal expectations wholesale, freeing younger generations from some of the antiquated assumptions we've faced."

That's the goal of *The New I Do*. We are providing you with a road map to create or re-create your marriage so it's successful by how you and you partner define success.

Ready to explore?

Chapter 2

WHY PUT A RING ON IT?

———————————————————

"Marriage is a wonderful institution,
but who wants to live in an institution?"
—Groucho Marx

*N*ow that we've explored the history of marriage and the sad state of marriage today, the question that we must ask is, "Why do you want to get married?" Especially now that we have essentially removed baby-making, sex, and financial dependence from marriage.

Do you believe marriage is just one of those things we do—go to college, get a job, get married? Do you feel pressured to marry by your parents or your religion, or because you've spent the past year being a bridesmaid at your friends' weddings? Do you want to have kids? Do you fear being alone? Do you want someone to take care of you? Do you want to marry for all those reasons and maybe a few more?

We're not going to judge your reasons for wanting to marry—people have been marrying for what others might consider the "wrong" reasons for centuries. As we saw in the last chapter, many marriages were for the benefit of everyone but the bride and groom. People don't marry like that anymore, thankfully, but that doesn't mean that their motivations for tying the knot will get them the kind of marriage they want if they don't change the paradigm. And that's what we're asking you to do—to stop believing that marriage has to look and be a certain way based on other people's beliefs, assumptions, and expectations.

Almost everyone who comes of age hears, "When are you going to get married?" at some point, but few—if any—hear, "*Why* do you want to get married?"

It isn't as easy to answer as you may think—unless you are following a life script you were not aware of. Your reason for marrying is probably not going to be the same at all ages and circumstances. If you're just getting out of college, do you think you're marrying for the same reason as a sixty-year-old empty-nester? If you're pushing thirty-five and want to have a child, are you marrying for the same reason as a couple that accidentally got pregnant? If you're a struggling forty-year-old single mom, are you marrying for the same reason as a financially secure CEO?

We want to help you identify more clearly why you want to get married—and whether or not you're even marriage material—and help you find a marital model that fits your reasons for marrying. That way, you will have a successful marriage by your definition of success—no one else's. We don't want you to end up like the 30 percent of divorced women who say they knew they were marrying the wrong man on their wedding day, according to *How Not to Marry the Wrong Guy* author Jennifer Gauvain. While no one has researched it as far as we can tell, we imagine a good portion of men feel the same way, too. How did so many women end up saying "I do" when they clearly didn't? According to Gauvain, the top reasons were:

1. We've dated for so long, and I don't want to waste all the time we have invested in the relationship.

2. I don't want to be alone.

3. He'll change after we get married.

4. It is too late, too embarrassing, and/or too expensive to call off the wedding.

5. He is a really nice guy; I don't want to hurt his feelings.

We agree that those are unhealthy reasons to tie the knot. However, marrying for companionship, especially if it's a more self-actualized way of solving the "I don't want to be alone" dilemma, is as good a reason as any for marrying, as you'll see later in the book. So let's explore the seemingly innocent question of why you want to get married.

If you answer by saying, "I want to get married for love," you certainly would not be the first to express that. The vast majority—93 percent, according to the Pew Research Center—believe that love is the number one reason to get married. After that comes making a lifelong commitment (87 percent), companionship (81 percent), having children (59 percent), and financial stability (31 percent).

Love, commitment, companionship, kids, finances—all of these sound familiar and make sense when people conceptualize what marriage is about. While those are the top reasons, there are a lot of other conscious and unconscious ideas that drive couples to say, "I do."

For instance, sex.

One woman who answered our survey of several hundred people said that, while she loves her husband, "[her] love for him was not [her] main reason for getting married." Her number one reason was to be able to have sex without sinning.

While interviewing engaged couples, we often ask each of them to separately list all the reasons they want to tie the knot. After, we ask them to read their list aloud to each other so they can have a discussion about expectations, especially differing expectations. Often, they list the same things, but not always. So when one groom-to-be read his reasons aloud, the look on his fiancée's face was priceless when he said, "to have sex."

"You want to marry *for sex?*" she asked, surprised.

He immediately turned somewhat sheepish as he attempted to

defend what felt natural and real for him: "Well, they asked us to check off *all* the reasons, so, um, yeah. . . ."

It's not that the bride-to-be didn't want or expect sex in her marriage; she just didn't see it as a compelling reason to get married. Was he wrong to want to list sex as part of the marital package? No. Was she wrong to have not placed the same value on sex in a marriage as he did? Of course not.

While we tend to agree that a satisfying sex life is an important aspect to marriage, we also acknowledge that others may not want to make that a priority or even a consideration, which we discuss in the chapter on Companionship Marriage. That's okay, too. And couples that feel that way may be onto something; as *Mating in Captivity* author and therapist Esther Perel says, passion and marriage cannot coexist, period. A passionate marriage, she writes, "is a contradiction in terms. Passion has always existed, but mostly outside the conjugal bed."

Still, that one brief uncomfortable moment in the two-plus hours we spent with the couple illuminates just how problematic differing marital expectations can be. The fact that she didn't see sex as a compelling reason to get married and that he did is surely worthy of a discussion, not only about sex but also about monogamy and even infidelity (more on those later). Isn't it better to address those expectations *before* you walk down the aisle together?

Yes, and here's why—there's a huge disconnect in how people conceptualize marriage and how they act once they're in it. While couples traditionally have vowed to be faithful and together forever, it's obvious that with a divorce rate of about 50 percent and infidelity rates that may be as high as 70 percent, those vows don't hold true. In fact, one study found that half of newlywed women said they expected infidelity would be part of their marriage, and 72 percent said they believed they'd experience divorce. What does that tell you?

Not that it's bad to mull over those possibilities. Having realistic expectations of marriage—including its darker side—may actually help couples. While it may seem weird to think that being overly optimistic about your marriage can cause problems, research by James McNulty, who runs Florida State University's Newlywed

Project Research Laboratory, indicates that it may lead newlyweds to feel disgruntled later on. What matters more, he says, is having accurate knowledge of your relationship's strengths and weaknesses.

That's why exploring your motivations for marrying as well as identifying what you're good at when it comes to your relationship are so important. It isn't okay to just assume that marriage is another thing on life's trajectory. But all too often, we hear that from the engaged couples we interview. "Marriage is just the next thing you do," one bride-to-be said as her fiancé nodded in agreement. "You graduate, you get a job, you get married." Another bride-to-be told us, "Our married friends just seem more adult," despite the fact that she and her fiancé have been living together, happily, for five years and are well established in their careers. What's not adult about that?

Despite the many ways to live and couple today, marriage has its pull. It's most likely what your parents hope for you, what many of your friends are doing, and what you may expect for yourself. Perhaps not surprisingly, having a lot of recently married friends can impact your own decision to marry. Whether or not you want to be "more adult," studies show that if your friends are getting hitched, you're more likely to wed soon, too. Again, these are not necessarily conscious decisions, although often they are—who wants to be different when everyone around you seems to be getting on with his or her life and planning for a future as a couple?

We hope you want to get married because it's something you're giving a lot of thought to, not just because you're bowing to internal and external expectations and pressure that you should marry, or that you see it as the only way to be an adult. Getting married is about the biggest decision you'll make in your life; it's way too important to let others dictate it for you.

So, why get married?

MARITAL PERKS AND MARITAL BUMMERS

Marriage isn't for everyone. That said, there are quite a few benefits to being married, otherwise we wouldn't have seen the incredible efforts by same-sex couples to be able to tie the knot in recent years.

Although marriage no longer serves the same purpose as it used to, as we saw in Chapter 1, it still matters to many of us. It's what sociologist Andrew Cherlin says is a capstone—"the last brick put in place after everything else is set"—and a status symbol.

Still, most would-be spouses really don't give a second thought to those things as reasons to marry; we don't know of any woman who says she wants to tie the knot because she wants a health boost or a way to avoid suicide (see sidebar on page 35). We imagine you don't either. We also don't know of anyone who marries in hopes that it will restrict her or his freedom, and yet that is exactly what traditional marriage does. On a certain level, it seems people acknowledge that reality. All you have to do is look at the typical bachelor and bachelorette party—brides- and grooms-to-be often celebrate their "last night of freedom" with off-the-wall sexual antics.

But sexual freedom (if not sexual desire) is not the only thing you give up when you marry. Some research indicates marriage limits social circles and may even disconnect you from your parents. Why does that happen? Perhaps not surprisingly, couples that live together, married or not, tend to want to spend time with each other. That, of course, takes away from whatever time they might spend with friends and family instead. Interestingly, couples that live together first and then marry tend to have even fewer get-togethers with friends than couples that just live together.

Plus, when you meld families and gain in-laws—mother-in-law jokes aside—things can get complicated. According to sociologist Deborah Merrill, whether you continue to have a good relationship with your family once you marry depends a lot on whom you marry—especially for men. Daughters-in-law have a lot of power in how close their husband remains to his family; they are much more likely to ask their husband to see less of his parents than sons-in-law are. Marriage may indeed be a "greedy institution."

Yet, people are willing to give up freedom, no matter how much they may value it, for commitment. Is there a way to incorporate that sense of freedom into a marriage? We believe it is possible. So did the late Peggy Vaughan. The author of *The Monogamy Myth*, who spoke

Many studies indicate that while it may not be perfect, marriage offers more good than bad. Here's what the research says:

- Marriage makes people happy (although other studies indicate that happy people tend to marry, and those who live together are actually happier and have better self-esteem than married couples).

- Married couples tend to create more wealth than singles (although with smart financial decisions, singles can do just fine).

- Married couples get more than 1,000 tax and government perks.

- People who are married at midlife may avoid premature death.

- Marriage makes us healthier (but it also tends to make us fatter, and unhappy marriages are stressful and increase the risk of depression or heart disease).

- Married men have a 46 percent lower rate of dying from cardiovascular disease than unmarried men, but wives who avoid conflict with their spouses have an increased risk of dying from any cause.

- Married people tend to have lower rates of mental illness and suicide, although marriage is less beneficial for those married to a mentally ill spouse.

- Married people are less likely to smoke or drink heavily, lifestyle changes known to lower rates of cardiovascular disease, cancer, and respiratory diseases.

- Kids tend to do better with two loving parents (although they don't have to actually be married, and much of that has to do with certain characteristics of those who choose to marry).

- Married people commit fewer crimes.

On the plus side, there are all sorts of legal benefits that affect everything from where people live to how they die to who can inherit their stuff to who will be able to make medical decisions for them to who can take family or bereavement leave. In other words, society gives married people *a lot* of perks, and couples in satisfying marriages feel pretty good about themselves—not to mention how happy they'll make their Grandma Betty, who has made it clear that she plans to stay alive as long as it takes to see them say their marital vows.

openly about getting past her husband's infidelities, believed that people would find more satisfaction in their marriage if they redefined what it means to be married. Without a balance of freedom and commitment, she warned, "the day will almost surely come when you will feel resentful at having given up so much, and you'll either leave the marriage or resign yourself to a deadened relationship."

That's why we are asking you to consider a different way of marrying, not a marriage that limits you or completes you, but a marriage that expands you and offers you freedom.

You'll be happier and more committed in your relationship if you have a partner who continually helps you become a better person, according to psychology professors Arthur Aron and Gary W. Lewandowski Jr., whose research focuses on self-expansion—the way people use relationships to gather knowledge and experiences throughout their life. In our survey, more than 90 percent agree that an ideal marriage is one that encourages mental, emotional, and spiritual growth in each other, and slightly more than 75 percent believe independence is necessary. We'd argue that independence should be at 90 percent, too.

So, if you're hung up on a marriage that completes you versus one that challenges you to grow, what you're really saying is that you are bringing an incomplete "you" to the marital table. Excuse us if this sounds rude, but do you really think being an incomplete person makes you good marriage material? While we don't have any top-ten list of what makes a person good marriage material or not, we believe it's important for you to examine all the attributes that you think make a "good wife" and a "good husband" according to the kind of marriage you want to have. Do wives and husbands have to do the same things to be seen as "good"? In what way do gendered expectations and stereotypes influence your beliefs?

Men and women seem to be pretty aligned on the traits that make a good partner in the marital model we have now. The top three for both are being a good parent, being caring and compassionate, and putting your family before anything else. After that comes being a good sexual partner, providing a good income, being well educated, and, finally, being good at household chores. But what you value in a partner will depend on what marital model is the best fit for you. You'll most certainly agree that being a good parent is essential if you want to have a Parenting Marriage. You may decide that being a good provider matters more than anything if you want a Safety Marriage. But being a good parent will have no relevance if you don't plan to have kids, just like being a good sexual partner may be the last thing on your mind if you want a Companionship Marriage or an Open Marriage. In other words, you will have to define what being good marriage material is by the kind of marriage you want to have.

That's especially important because men and women typically don't experience marriage the same way, which sociologist Jessie Bernard observed in the 1970s. What she concluded, and which other scholars more recently have corroborated, is that there isn't really one marriage—there's a "his" and "her" marriage, depending on whether you are the wife or the husband. Women still tend to be responsible for the emotional work in a marriage—the planning, organizing, and structuring of family life, as well as the unpaid (and all too often unnoticed and unappreciated) caring work for friends, extended family, schools, and religious and other community organizations—which frequently leaves them exhausted and frustrated. Not only that, but wives still are responsible for the bulk of the household chores even though husbands nowadays do more than our fathers and grandfathers did.

Poet Jill Bialosky knowingly acknowledged what many women feel: "I had wanted to get married, but I realized now that I had never wanted to be 'a wife.'"

That doesn't mean men haven't struggled within the confines of being husbands. Having to conform to societal pressure to be breadwinners—and 41 percent of men and women still think that's an important quality for a man to be a good husband or partner—means that men don't have a lot of wiggle room to meet their needs in the traditional marital model either.

Can men and women get their needs met in a marriage while committing to the union?

WHAT ABOUT THE "C" WORD?

Let's talk about commitment, which is the second reason people list for marrying on the Pew study. Like love, it isn't that easily defined, although almost everyone has a general idea of what it means: committed couples care, not only about each other, but also about the relationship itself; they compromise and sacrifice; they put their partners before themselves; they don't give up when things get hard; they are willing to do whatever it takes to make the relationship work (which is the same as acknowledging that, sorry, you're not always going to have your way, and, yes, you will have to sacrifice).

For many, commitment means you stay together forever no matter what. Every engaged couple we've worked with emphatically stated how much they value commitment and how important it will be in their marriage. It's hard to argue with that, especially when it's stated so passionately. Yet when we asked them what they won't tolerate in their marriage, it's clear commitment only goes so far and stops—perhaps not surprisingly—at addiction, abuse, and infidelity.

In the case of infidelity, however, it's not always so clear-cut. "What if it was just a one-night stand?" we asked.

After an uncomfortable silence, most of the brides- and grooms-to-be softened. "Well, *maybe* we can work through that."

"How about a long-term affair?" we asked.

"Absolutely not!"

"Multiple one-nighters?"

"No way!"

It's clear sexual fidelity plays a huge part in society's idea of commitment. Should it? Some believe other things should be valued much more, like kindness and consideration. Would kindness and consideration be enough for you to be happily married instead of insisting on 100 percent sexual fidelity? (More on that in Chapter 9.)

Commitment appears to be flexible, not static. Is it a choice? Many believe it is, but people's ideas about commitment may be less about making a choice than internalizing societal pressure to maintain relationships. How often do you read that people need to "work" on a marriage? How often have you heard that couples that split weren't committed enough or just didn't understand what commitment means? In truth, most people have several committed relationships before they settle down.

We agree that commitment is important in a healthy marriage. We also ask you to consider where you want to draw the line. You've already seen that commitment often hits a wall when it comes to affairs, addictions, and abuse. So it's essential that you're clear about what you're committing to and your motivations for doing so.

That may matter more than ever since people live so much longer than in generations past. Sacrificing when life expectancy was somewhere between forty and fifty years and when marriages lasted twenty to thirty years, as in the 1900s, is a lot different than sacrificing when people are living to eighty, ninety, one hundred years, as many do now, with couples frequently marking seventy-five years-plus together. What will commitment look like if projections that people, perhaps even you, will live healthy, productive lives for 150 years or more come true?

WHAT IS MARRIAGE ANYWAY?

We've been talking about marriage as if all of us are in complete agreement about what it actually is. So, it seems like a good time to ask you what you know about marriage and why you know it. Take a moment to read the following sentence. Then write down the first thing that comes to your mind.

Marriage is _____.

Now, let's see if we're all still in agreement. Strip away romance and the idea of love, soul mates, and the fairy tale of "happily-ever-after," and what you'll discover is that at its core, marriage is a legal contract. That's what a marriage license is. Although priests, ministers, rabbis, and other religious officials marry people all the time, and, while some religious institutions won't perform or even recognize a marriage under certain circumstances, you don't need to have a religious ceremony to be married. All you need to do is go to your county clerk, pay for a marriage license, gather an officiate and some witnesses, and that's it—no stressing over the gown, the color of the bridesmaids' dresses, the bouquet, the DJ, the venue, the cake, the guest list, and myriad other details that mark today's often over-the-top wedding ceremonies. It's actually a pretty simple legal contract, if not necessarily a simple emotional contract.

By marrying, you not only make a public statement of your commitment but you also are combining your home, family, and social and financial structures. In essence, marriage is a business deal. And the best way to protect those going into a business deal is to have a prenup.

Gulp! We know—there is nothing about a prenup that sounds even remotely romantic, and much of what you hear about prenups is that they're forced upon someone, often the bride-to-be, by the wealthier person at the last minute, thus putting one person at a great disadvantage.

That obviously is not what we're talking about. More people are seeing the value of them; the American Academy of Matrimonial Lawyers says prenups are up 73 percent in the past five years, and more women are requesting them, perhaps because more women have economic power nowadays. And since we are exploring new ways to enter into a marital contract, prenups make sense because they get couples to talk about what they want from the marriage. In truth, every married couple already has a prenup, whether they signed up for it or not. Each state's laws on marriage and divorce are basically prenups, so you can either use your state's or you can create your own.

Also gaining interest is the postnup, which is like a prenup in that the couple addresses what they want from a marriage, but postnups come after a couple is already married. While we believe prenups are essential for creating the marital model that will set you up for success, postnups may also make sense when unforeseen events occur in a marriage, like infidelity or an inheritance, or when children come along. In fact, having children almost demands a prenup because family law does not recognize all the caretaking, household chores, trips to doctors and dentists, and hours spent on school projects that anyone who stays at home with the kids faces. That's why the prenup between rapper-entrepreneur Jay-Z and singer Beyoncé, both multimillionaires on their own, gives her $5 million for each child they have together in recognition of whatever income she'll lose while pregnant and raising the kids.

"I would encourage any woman getting married to put on such a treaty; it will gain more influence on self-esteem," Beyoncé advises. She's right, although we would argue that men should consider a cash-for-caregiving contract, too, in case he's the one who stays home.

Increasingly, prenups and postnups are being created for reasons that have nothing to do with the historical reason for them—money and property. Prenups have been created concerning fidelity, frozen embryos, chores, smoking, sex, drug testing, in-laws, and frequent-flier miles. While some of them may seem silly and may not be enforceable, they again indicate that not every couple has the same marriage and needs. Couples make all sorts of arrangements within their marriage—he stays home with the kids while she brings home the bacon, she does the laundry and gardening while he cooks and takes charge of paying the bills. That is the stuff of daily living. The bigger issues, the ones that will get you the kind of marriage you want, require more than just an informal agreement. They need a contract. (We talk more about prenups and postnups in Chapter 10).

Ignorance is not bliss, especially when it comes to one of the biggest decisions you'll make in your life—marriage. So should you understand *exactly* what your legal requirements are before saying, "I do"? We say yes. You probably wouldn't consider going into business with someone without the advice of a lawyer and maybe an accountant. Protections and guarantees would be discussed, agreed upon, and included in the contract. In other words, you and your business partner would know exactly what you're getting into.

We agree with David Allen Green, legal correspondent for the *New Statesman*, when he says, "the world would be a far happier place if marriage was harder and divorce easier. There would be far fewer divorce lawyers if there were more marriage lawyers, just as companies that are realistic and well-advised when they negotiate a contract tend not to get bogged down subsequently in messy litigation."

Or, as history professor Glenda Riley says, "We're putting a waiting period on guns. Marriage is as volatile a situation as purchasing a weapon; yet, people can get married in three days."

That may mean that fewer couples might choose to marry, but those that tied the knot anyway might truly live up to their vows. We're not quite sure how making marriage harder would work, nor are we convinced that it should be harder. Would a waiting period be enough? Should you have to be a certain age; earn a certain income; have a life plan; undergo mandatory premarital counseling; take some sort of test; attend parenting classes; learn how to communicate and deal with conflict better; or all of the above? It's complicated.

But that doesn't get you—a future bride- or groom-to-be—off the hook for taking responsibility for understanding the legal realities you're signing up for when you decide to marry. Nor should you enter into an institution without questioning why you're doing it.

"Too often we are presented with the false choice between a life-long, loving marriage and a lonely, unmarried life. But those are far from the only options," say sociologists Laurie Essig and Lynn Owens. "When there is broad, seemingly unanimous support for an institution, and when the institution is propped up by such disparate ideas as love, civil rights, and wealth creation, we should wonder why so many different players seem to agree so strongly. Perhaps it's because they are supporting not just marriage but also the status quo."

Think about it.

IS MARRIAGE RIGHT FOR ME?

Wondering if you're cut out for marriage? Here are a few questions you might want to ask yourself:

- What are my reasons for marrying?
- Why do I want to get married instead of live together?
- Would I be more content being single?

- What do I think I'd give up by marrying?
- What do I think I'd gain by marrying?
- What does commitment mean to me?
- How important is commitment in a marriage?
- What behaviors would I not be able to tolerate in marriage?
- When I think of what married life is like, what does it look like?
- What do I think I'll like about it?
- What won't I like about it?
- Why would it be easier or better than remaining single?
- Why might it be harder or worse?
- Do I believe marriage is "work"?
- How important is sexual fidelity?
- Was I ever tempted to be sexually unfaithful, and why?
- Do I believe I can be monogamous for the rest of my life?
- How important is love in a marriage?
- Do I know anyone who married for reasons other than love?
- Are there "right" and "wrong" reasons to marry?
- What do I think about divorce?
- What would make me consider divorce?
- Do I believe it's better to stay in an unhappy marriage "for the kids' sake" or divorce?
- What would be the ideal marriage, one in which I could keep the best of what I have now melded with commitment to another person?
- How will I know when I'm ready to marry?

Chapter 3

STARTER MARRIAGE:

TRYING ON MARRIAGE TO SEE IF IT FITS

"A successful marriage is an edifice that must be rebuilt every day."
—Andrea Maurois

Remember Vicki's hippie wedding in the wilds of the Rocky Mountains when she was twenty years old? Her first marriage was a Starter Marriage, although it was by default, not by choice. And that's how it happens for a lot of people; you think you're ready to be married—or feel pressured to say "I do"—and end up in a situation that unravels quickly, sometimes in under a year.

A Starter Marriage is pretty much what it sounds like—a test marriage of just a few years with no kids. They've been around for generations, but few have openly talked about them until noted anthropologist Margaret Mead began promoting the concept of trial marriages in the 1960s. Observing that one relationship may not be able to make it from the early romance and passion phase through the parenting phase and all its responsibilities (and sheer exhaustion) to the last few decades of life, in which companionship and caregiving are more valued, she suggested that time-limited, renegotiable contracts and serial monogamy might give men and women what they need. Why worry about how long a marriage lasts, she asked, when it really only matters if children are involved? It might be easy to write that off as some bad 1960s hippie-ish thinking, but, for the most part, people still feel and act that way; after all, don't people often tell childfree couples that divorce (often to their disdain), "Well, at least you didn't have kids"?

The concept of a temporary marriage has popped in and out of vogue since then, but it created the most buzz when journalist Pamela Paul's book *The Starter Marriage and the Future of Matrimony* was published in 2002. While Paul believed many of her thirty-something peers wed while "mesmerized by the romantic idea of marriage and blinded to the reality," she didn't view these short-lived marriages as a bunch of "failed" marriages—not unlike Mead's recognition of serial monogamy. Instead, she found that there was an upside to them: "Like a starter home, a starter marriage can teach you a lot about what to look for, and what to avoid, the next time around." Indeed, most of the people she interviewed expected to marry again, this time with a newfound perspective. A Starter Marriage is a "learner marriage," says Sascha Rothchild, author of *How to Get Divorced by 30*.

That's why we're in favor of Starter Marriages. Now, this doesn't mean that we encourage you to marry the "wrong" person or just anyone for the sake of being married, and it doesn't mean that you should marry in *hopes* of it ending by a certain time. What's the point of that? It also isn't so you can check off "get married" from your to-do list (which you shouldn't do anyway when it comes to something as important as marriage). The idea is to choose someone you actually *want* to marry because he or she has a lot of what you're looking for in a mate. You're just not going to vow, "until death do us part." Instead, you will agree to be together in a renewable contract for two, three, four, or more years—whatever works for you and your partner. But no matter what terms you and your partner agree to commit to, and no matter what goals you set for the marriage, one is a must—neither of you should have a child and you must agree not to have kids (although you might want to keep the marriage short and sweet depending on your age, especially if you eventually want to have children). It's a bad idea to "try on" marriage with young lives in the balance, according to the research by Andrew Cherlin, author of *The Marriage-Go-Round: The State of Marriage and Family in America Today*. He points to studies that suggest the children often develop behavioral problems if they experience a parade of new partners moving in and out of their lives.

REINING IN "UNTIL DEATH DO US PART"

Let's step back first and fully consider the odd concept of a renewable marriage contract or what some call a "wedlease." Agreeing to be married for a limited amount of time seems downright strange, perhaps even offensive. Love doesn't have an expiration date, you may be thinking; why not start off with a promise to love each other forever? Wouldn't placing a time limit on a relationship be basically saying that you're unable or unwilling to commit and work on a relationship from the get-go? Wouldn't it mean that you would always be aware that you had an easy out in the back of your mind, and any perceived or real infraction would be enough to send you packing?

The cap's off the toothpaste tube—*again?* Out of here!

Can't get him to stop playing *Grand Theft Auto V*? Gone!

Another pair of black shoes? How many does the woman need? Hasta la vista, baby!

Okay, those are pretty unlikely scenarios to send a couple to splitsville (although the money spent on the black shoes just might cause irreparable tension, since couples tend to fight more about money than anything else). Still, time limits don't seem to fit in with our vision of "what marriage should look like." That, of course, is our point. We need to stop seeing marriage through a narrow lens. Marriage doesn't have to be an "until death do us part" agreement (which is still a contract with an expiration date: death). Marriage should be considered "successful" by what it has accomplished, not by how long it lasts. If people are going to continue to see marriage that way, then, yes—a renewable contract is going to create quite a bit of angst for many of them. It doesn't seem "romantic," although we believe it's a statement of true love and commitment to say, "I do," over again to your partner by renewing your marriage contract. It's a conscious decision that you want to make your partnership last, and you might decide on some things you both need to do better. It's also sending a message that you're in the marriage because you *choose* to be, not because you *have* to be. Isn't that why some people renew their vows? Renewing a marital contract is no different, although it's a lot more binding than vows.

"But what if my partner doesn't want to renew?" you may be wondering. That is a valid concern, although, let's face it—that already happens in our traditional marriage model. It's called divorce, and about 10 percent of first marriages don't make it to the fifth year. A marriage license does not guarantee that you or your spouse will remain happy, faithful, or married. Nor do the vows you say when you stand before your loved one. Very few people, if anyone, tie the knot with divorce in mind; most people don't want or expect it to happen (although a surprisingly large number of newlywed women, 74 percent, admit they wouldn't be shocked if it did happen). Yet people divorce and many marry again, sometimes several times; humans are serial monogamists, otherwise everyone would still be with the first person he or she fell in love with (admittedly, there are some people who are). That doesn't mean that people are any less committed while they are in those partnerships: as one researcher discovered, "if anything, there is more commitment in more relationships, and the commitment that is being experienced is taking on a different form."

Because men and women are marrying later nowadays, they have many more years to experience numerous committed relationships and many more chances to explore who they are with different partners. What we like about a Starter Marriage is that it can help couples align expectations, create a plan of what each partner will contribute to the marriage, clarify goals, and strategize what will happen if one or both don't want to renew the contract. Waiting until death when you already feel that you're dying in a marriage isn't helping anyone achieve a healthy and satisfying partnership.

ADDRESSING THE "MARRIAGE PROBLEM"

We certainly aren't the first to suggest the idea of a marital contract. Marriage contracts of five years were allowed (and were, interestingly, rarely dissolved) in ancient Japan. German Romantic poet Johann von Goethe entertained the idea in 1809 in his *Elective Affinities*. Paleontologist E. D. Cope, writing in *The Marriage Problem* in 1888, suggested that every marriage should start with a five-year contract that either party could end, followed by a ten- or fifteen-year contract that both spouses would have to agree to end, and finally a permanent contract—a system he believed would provide "a safe opportunity for the correction of errors in matrimony, and a chance for the reorganization and recommencement on a more hopeful basis of the lives of persons who have made such mistakes." But beginning with a five-year Starter Marriage contract, he believed, "would furnish the experience necessary to a better understanding of the relation, and of a better line of conduct in practical life."

In the mid-1920s, Denver juvenile court judge and social reformer Ben B. Lindsey proposed—to much outrage—what he called a "companionate marriage" (not to be confused with what we consider companionate marriages to be today), a form of legalized marriage for young people that included access to sex education and birth control as well as divorce by mutual consent. The couple could have sex, but no kids, and would be able to easily split if things didn't work out, or they could convert their marriage into a "family" marriage if things did. He was promptly booted from the bench after an illustrious twenty-eight-year career.

In 1971, Lena King Lee, an African-American Maryland legislator, proposed a Marriage-Contractual Renewal Bill. Wanting to help young adults avoid problems in future marriages, she proposed that marriages could be annulled or renewed every three years—a proposal that brought her national attention and appearances on the *Today Show* and elsewhere. It didn't pass, but her efforts helped usher in the adoption of no-fault divorce in the state.

More recently, lawmakers in Mexico City, which houses a Catholic population with a high divorce rate, explored the idea of a limited marital contract. A few years ago, a handful of lawmakers proposed a reform to the civil code to allow couples to decide on the length of their commitment, with a minimum marriage of two years (which is about when a good portion of Mexico City residents generally decide to end their marriages). While the proposal eventually died, it certainly got a lot of people—there and abroad—talking about the idea of renewable marriage contracts. In 2010, a women's group in the Philippines proposed a ten-year marital contract as well, except in this case, if a couple didn't renew their marriage—or somehow forgot to—their marriage would automatically be null and void.

It's evident that many people over many decades have noticed that the lifelong marital contract does not stop people from leaving a marriage they want to leave. While none of those proposals passed as legislation, there's no reason why you can't create your own marital contract. Some states already offer a legal alternative marital contract, a Covenant Marriage, which we will talk about later in the book.

But a contract with just a time limit alone won't help you create the marriage you want—a marriage that sets you up for success according to how you define success. Not every couple wants the same thing from their romantic commitments. People marry for all sorts of reasons, and they should be free and encouraged to create a couple-specific contract that guides their lives together based on what they consider important. Some people suggest that, if each couple was expected and required to personalize their marriage contract, tailored to their own needs, there would be no societal stigma or judgment over what are essentially private decisions.

COHABITATION IS NOT LIKE MARRIAGE

So, if the idea of marriage contracts has been around for centuries and society *still* hasn't embraced it, why should anyone embrace it now? While marriage has been many things and has served many purposes over time, as you've seen in the first chapter, never before has marriage been at such a crossroads. With more states allowing marriage between same-sex couples, with only a small percentage of all families following the nuclear family model, with more people delaying marriage or rejecting it, and with more people living together before marriage, we believe society is perfectly positioned to change the rules of marriage so that it's not an off-the-shelf contract.

You might be wondering, "Why should I even bother with a Starter Marriage when I can give marriage a 'test run' by living together first? Why should I deal with the hassle of the paperwork and the expense and hoopla of a wedding?" Those are reasonable questions, especially since many couples are doing just that. There are about 15.3 million unmarried heterosexual couples living together today, and many more same-sex couples, and it does not look like it's going to stop any time soon. So, here's our answer: Cohabitation, while similar to marriage, is not the same as marriage. First of all, you don't have the same legal and financial protections. That's huge, but beyond that, people act differently while cohabiting. Couples often have different expectations while living together, and their friends, family, coworkers, and society in general view them differently—they aren't even seen as being a family by 47 percent of unmarried adults.

Not sure about that? Well, consider this—what comes to mind when you hear the words "wife" and "husband"? Do you have a mental picture of what it means to be a "wife" or a "husband" (and please be aware if you find yourself falling into gendered role expectations)? Now, what comes to mind when you hear "cohabiting couple"? That's a little more confusing, right? There's no way to easily define what a cohabiting couple looks or acts like or what role the guy or gal has (we're obviously talking about hetero couples; for same-sex couples, there are no gendered expectations and thus they luckily escape the scrutiny hetero couples face). That's not necessarily a bad thing. In fact, cohabiting couples tend to be more gender egalitarian.

Men don't "have" to be breadwinners—more cohabiting women have jobs than their partners—and they still have someone to clean the house and their clothes (yes, cohabiting women tend to do more of that than the guys). But much of that has to do with socioeconomic issues as well as whether the couple intends to marry at some point, as about 40 percent do within three years of moving in together. Unlike cohabitation, marriage encourages specialization—it's a lot more effective if a couple divides and conquers: One person takes care of the children and house, and another works outside the house to support the family. Not only that, but society has certain expectations about how a wife and a husband act, and most people internalize those expectations. Society has come a long way from the days when a wife was a homemaker who cared for the kids, whipped up a casserole for dinner, and had a cold martini waiting for her husband, the man who'd been slaving away at the office all day because he was the breadwinner. Marriage is much more flexible nowadays, thankfully, but many people still struggle with deep-seated gendered expectations and beliefs. Who gets in trouble when your mother-in-law doesn't get a thank-you note? Who buys the Christmas and Hanukkah presents and plans the Thanksgiving get-togethers and family birthday parties? For the most part, those responsibilities still fall under the domain of "wife."

Not only are roles fuzzy for cohabiters; the reasons for cohabiting often can be just as problematic, especially if the couple has different expectations. He may see it as a temporary arrangement to save on expenses, while she may see it as a step toward marriage, or vice versa. What you don't want to do is end up marrying just because you've been living together for a few years and it seems like the next logical thing to do or because of inertia—what marriage researcher Scott Stanley has called "sliding" into marriage. Since one of the most important goals of this book is to help people marry smarter and more consciously, please—no sliding.

All of which means, if you truly want to explore what being married is like, living together won't really give you the answer. Having a Starter Marriage with a contract, however, will. And it will make you smarter and more prepared for either the renewal of your marital contract or a new marriage with a new partner.

STARTER = SMARTER

The title of this section is what *The Starter Marriage* author Pamela Paul discovered in her research. "Those coming out of starter marriages really learn about themselves, how they function in a relationship, about what marriage really means."

And that's what Thorin Klosowski, a thirty-one-year-old

Colorado writer, experienced, too, when he married his live-in girl-friend of some four years. "On the surface, my marriage had all the makings of something that should work: no infidelity, no abuse, and we seemingly got along great," he says.

Despite that, the marriage lasted three years, but he discovered a lot more about relationships, good partnerships, and the importance of honesty in that short time. "If there's something that's off the table and you can't discuss it, then you need to be paying a little more attention to it," he says. "We were ignoring a lot of things and not dealing with them. Looking back at it, it's almost hilarious how we were kind of blindly going through this."

For Klosowski and his then-wife, there were a few big issues they skirted around—like having kids. They had talked about having children before they wed, but he wasn't too keen on having them, at least at that point, and he made that known. But even he assumed that once he graduated college and they got hitched, he'd change his mind. "It just never happened," he says. In hindsight, Klosowski realizes he kept avoiding the "when are we having kids" conversation because he had a gut feeling that the marriage wasn't going to last.

His Starter Marriage illuminated what the years they spent living together did not. He openly says that, when they were living together, he always felt that he had an easy out (of course, he also had an easy out of the marriage, too—aka divorce—as he now realizes). By the time they went for marriage counseling, it was too late for the marriage, but it awakened him to his own roadblocks.

"It put me in the position of taking relationships a lot more seriously, a lot more forward thinking. It made me think bigger and broader. In the end, when it was over, it taught me to pay a hell of a lot more attention to my own emotions than I ever was before. That was the big thing I wasn't addressing or talking about with her or even thinking about myself. It was like, 'Okay, I like this person. She's my best friend. Of course we're going to get married.' I never thought about the deeper emotional issues that needed to be addressed. Now I definitely do."

Klosowski would like to marry again, but, next time, he'll follow his own advice: keep talking about expectations and what each of you is willing to do—or not—for the marriage, and pay attention to what you're not addressing and why. If Klosowski and his former wife had entered into a Starter Marriage as we envision it, he would not have been able to "kind of blindly [go] through" their partnership. They may have decided not to renew their contract anyway—especially since they were far apart on the question of whether or not to have children—but it wouldn't be because they hadn't clarified what they hoped to accomplish by marrying.

Sascha Rothchild had similar revelations. She married at twenty-seven and divorced two years later. There were a lot of reasons that it didn't work, even beyond the fact that after two years of dating and a year of living together, she had to nag her boyfriend into proposing. She married the wrong guy (a "laid-back, lovable stoner") for the wrong reasons (she was on a self-created fabricated deadline, and all her friends were getting hitched) at the wrong time (she was emotionally unavailable). Not surprisingly, the marriage was not salvageable. To her credit, instead of pointing fingers, Rothchild began exploring in therapy what she was bringing to the marital table. She realized she had some issues she needed to get under control.

"I went into it really not knowing what it takes to have a good marriage. I didn't know the amount of work, how well you need to communicate, how to really share your life with someone," she told us.

Now married to a man who agreed to go to therapy with her to work on their challenges—after just three months of dating—the thirty-seven-year-old Los Angeles resident says, "I learned so much about myself . . . I could not be where I am now had I not learned that having been married and divorced."

Her advice? "Really think about why you made certain decisions, and change, make some changes with yourself."

If Rothchild had tied the knot with a Starter Marriage as we envision it, she wouldn't have been unclear about "what it takes to have a good marriage" because she and her then husband-to-be would have had to actually define and agree on what a "good marriage" looks like. It's too easy for people to imagine that things will change for the better or become clearer just because they are now Mr. and Mrs.

Although many newlyweds will tell you that marriage "changes things," what they really mean is that there is a shift in consciousness as the idea of being someone's "wife" or "husband" sinks in. And just about every newlywed gets somewhat rattled by that. "There's a bit of a shock that happens afterward, when the party is over and all of a sudden a marriage begins and there are all of these unanswered questions," says Kim Perel, co-editor of the anthology *Wedding Cake for Breakfast: Essays on the Unforgettable First Year of Marriage*. "Many couples are living together now before they get married, and they think nothing will change, but really, marriage does change things."

The kind of changes Rothchild is talking about are different. If you didn't handle conflict well as boyfriend and girlfriend (or boyfriend and boyfriend or girlfriend and girlfriend), it's not going to suddenly get better just because you're married. If she was a bit of a slob while you were living together, marriage will not magically transform her into a domestic goddess.

The "unanswered questions" Perel wonders about are how a couple creates a life together. Can you answer those "unanswered questions," have that kind of self-awareness Rothchild described, and work on your issues (we are sure you have some; we do) before you walk down the aisle? Yes, although let's be real—living with another person 24/7 often brings up unconscious behaviors and deep-seated beliefs you probably weren't even aware of that may clash with your partner's behaviors and beliefs. No contract is going to be able to anticipate every future possibility. Nonetheless, a Starter Marriage with a detailed contract enables you and your partner to become much more aligned and focused than a vague vow about "better and worse" and "until death do us part" can ever offer.

A Starter Marriage may not be for everyone, however. It probably isn't a good fit if deadlines cause you to get defiant or lazy—allowing others to make decisions for you—or if you have a tendency to ignore things in hopes that they will go away (which, of course, they won't). It certainly isn't going to work for people who measure a marriage's success by how long it lasts instead of what it accomplishes and what the couple can learn from it while it lasts.

SAMPLE STARTER MARRIAGE CONTRACT

Because every marriage contract will be unique to the needs, goals, and desires of the two people entering into it, there is no blanket contract that will fit everyone. But to give you an example of what a marriage contract might look like, we have created a fictional couple that live in Boulder, Colorado—Romeo, thirty-one, a high school English teacher with a yearly salary of $49,000, and Juliet, twenty-eight, a social media marketing manager for a nonprofit with a yearly salary of $52,000. Because they both eventually want to have one child, they are keeping their contract short because Juliet wants to be sure she'll have plenty of time to factor in potential infertility problems or to find a new partner should they not renew their contract. They are planning a small wedding that their parents and stepparents have agreed to mostly pay for and a short honeymoon that they are paying for. They plan to continue to live in the one-bedroom apartment that they have been sharing with their dog, Rosaline, and for which both names are on the month-to-month rental agreement.

***

I, Romeo, and I, Juliet, enter into this marriage contract that goes into effect on June 5, 2015, the day of our wedding. The contract will be in effect for exactly two years, until June 5, 2017, at which point we will either convert our contract to a Parenting Marriage contract or dissolve the marriage.

We agree that we will each keep our surnames.

We agree to have monthly check-ins to assess our marriage and where we are in our goals. We agree to be transparent and honest about each assessment and agree to mutually pay for a neutral third party if needed.

We agree that we will discuss/decide whether to renew the contract or dissolve the marriage on or by January 5, 2017, giving us plenty of time to prepare for either scenario.

PURPOSE

In addition to making a public statement about our commitment to each other, we agree that the goals of our marriage are financial security, companionship, and helping each other grow as individuals and as a couple. We are seeking to create an egalitarian, honest, and mutually satisfying union.

FINANCES

We have fully revealed to each other our complete financial information, including our net worth, income, holdings, assets, and liabilities.

We agree to share equally all our household expenses, including rent, utilities, food, household supplies, décor and furnishings, and pet care, and will set up a joint checking account before June 5, 2015, in which we will each deposit $2,000 a month. Either of us can write checks on the account, but it may not be for personal use. We agree to balance the account together monthly.

We agree to pay off our portion of the wedding and honeymoon from our joint checking account.

We agree to have a joint credit card before June 5, 2015, for shared household and entertainment expenses that we will pay off in its entirety every month.

We agree that no purchase by cash, check, or credit card over $200 may be made without the other's knowledge and agreement.

We agree to deposit $1,000 a month each in a savings account with the goal of eventually having enough for a down payment on a house.

Juliet is solely responsible for paying off her student loan, which at the time of our wedding will be $20,000.

In the event that either of us loses our job or takes a job at a lower pay, we agree to reassess our financial situation and savings requirements.

We agree to pay for our own hobbies, solo entertainment, reading materials, clothes, toiletries (such as makeup, shaving supplies, etc.), grooming needs (haircuts, waxing, etc.), dry cleaning, gym memberships, and sports equipment (except for shared outdoor activities such as camping).

We agree to file our federal and state taxes jointly and to use our joint checking account to pay any taxes due. In the event of a refund, we agree to put it in our savings account.

In the event that we do not renew this contract, we agree that there will be no spousal support. We also agree to equally split our savings and whatever is left over in our joint checking account minus the cost of paying off mutual credit card debt and whatever costs are involved with dissolving the marriage. We agree to stop using the joint credit card and checking account immediately upon deciding not to renew the marital contract; any and all unexplained expenses will be the responsibility of the purchaser.

We agree to pay off any personal credit card debts monthly so that neither is responsible for each other's debt. We agree to share monthly personal credit card statements with each other.

We agree that any assets and holdings (such as IRAs, pension plans, stocks, bonds, mutual funds) each of us brings into the marriage belong to us separately if the contract is not renewed and the marriage dissolves.

HOUSEHOLD

We agree that we will equally share the costs and physical labor of all household chores, including but not limited to cleaning, food and household goods shopping, car maintenance, laundry, gardening/plant maintenance, and pet care, to an agreed-upon minimum cleanliness level even during any periods of unemployment, underemployment, and vacation time. Romeo prefers to be the chef for all dinners and parties, and Juliet is fine with that.

We agree to equally share in the emotional caretaking in this union, including but not limited to arranging and preparing for family and other social gatherings, responding to invitations, gift and greeting card purchasing, writing thank-yous, and contacting in-laws and family members.

We agree that due to the space limitations of our apartment, we will not have guests, whether family or friends, stay with us regardless of the duration or circumstance.

We agree that, if we do not renew this marital contract, Juliet will have the option of remaining in the apartment; if she chooses not to stay, then Romeo will have the option. The security deposit and any accrued interest will be split equally.

We agree that if we do not renew this marital contract, we will each take whatever furnishings we brought into the union and split whatever we acquired together or was given as a gift evenly, with the exception of the silverware set that was from Juliet's great-grandparents and the cast-iron pans that were from Romeo's grandmother.

HEALTH

We agree that we will do everything in our power to not get pregnant during this time; however, if we do, we agree to immediately enter into a Parenting Marriage contract.

We agree to share the costs of Juliet's birth control pills or any other birth control method as well as the costs of freezing and storing Juliet's eggs, which she will have 100 percent ownership over in the event the contract is not renewed and the marriage dissolves.

We agree to each have a life insurance policy of $100,000 that names each other as the beneficiary. We agree to each have a living trust and will and an advance directive.

We agree to use our joint checking account for medical and dental expenses, including co-pays and expenses not covered by insurance, except any elective cosmetic procedures.

We agree to require and mutually pay for each other to seek help/attend rehab in the event of any addiction.

We agree to require and mutually pay for any mental health needs, including but not limited to marital counseling, in the case of a medical diagnosis (such as bipolar disorder) or marital problems/concerns.

SEX

We agree that a healthy sex life is an important part of our union. We agree to be open, honest, and accommodating about our sexual needs and desires, and we agree to follow the GGG principle: giving, good, and game.

We agree to be sexually monogamous except in the event of a permanent disability that makes one of us unable to have intercourse, in which case we agree that the non-disabled person may have his/her sexual needs taken care of outside the marriage.

We agree to keep the conversation about monogamy and sexual needs and desires open and honest throughout the duration of this contract.

We agree that infidelity includes not only intercourse but also any emotional and/or sexual connection to a third party that is kept hidden from the other spouse, including but not limited to sexting. We agree that, in the event of infidelity, we will seek marital and individual counseling before making any decision (unilaterally or jointly) that would alter the contract.

CAREERS/EDUCATION

We agree to mutually decide upon any career change that might involve moving or a big decrease in salary.

In the event of a layoff or firing, we agree that the unemployed person must seek full-time employment first before opting for part-time work. If self-employment is an option, we must both agree that the benefits outweigh the risks before pursuing the work.

We agree that neither of our careers takes priority over the other's, and neither will be forced to move for a new career opportunity.

We agree that we will contribute equally for any future educational/ career development expenses, including costs for any related travel, books, supplies, etc.

PET

We agree to share equally in the care and all costs of our dog, Rosaline.

We agree to not add any more pets at this time.

We agree that we will have fifty-fifty shared custody of our dog, Rosaline, in the event that the contract is not renewed and the marriage is dissolved, and we will each pay for her care. We also agree that we will each have the right of first refusal to watch her instead of putting her in the care of a kennel or paid/unpaid dog-sitter.

FREE TIME

We agree to mutually decide where and when we will spend vacations, how much to spend, and how we will pay for any joint vacation.

We agree to discuss any travel each of us may want to take solo or with others for recreation or family purposes on his or her own. Any solo travel is the financial responsibility of the traveler.

We agree that time alone, or with friends or family, is important to each of us. We agree to support and encourage each other's free time, and we agree to set aside time each week to talk about upcoming private or shared social events.

We agree to spend no more than four days over the Christmas holiday with Romeo's family in Austin, Texas, and the four-day Thanksgiving holiday with Juliet's family in Colorado Springs. We will share all related travel expenses.

***

We acknowledge that we are intentionally choosing a Starter Marriage and would not enter into this marriage except for this marital contract in its present form.

We acknowledge that we are entering into this marital contract of our free will, and that we each have had separate legal counsel review our agreement.

We agree that we are committed to this marriage for the term outlined, and that we will do everything in our power to follow this marital contract.

We agree that if the marriage does not take place, this contract is null and void.

Husband:

Signed _____

Date _____

Wife:

Signed _____

Date _____

Witness:

Signed _____

Date _____

Witness:

Signed _____

Date _____

IF YOU RENEW

Well, congratulations! You made it through the years you agreed to stay together and presumably achieved some if not all of your goals. Before you renew your contract, you should plan with your partner where you want to go with your marriage next:

- Do you want to have kids, thus headed for a Parenting Marriage?
- Was monogamy a challenge, making an Open Marriage an attractive alternative?
- Maybe you have big plans that require you to step out of the work world for a while and you want to transform your union into a Safety Marriage.

Regardless of which marital model you plan to explore next, you will once again need to create new goals and agree to a new plan of action. The rest of the chapters in the book will steer you in the right direction, and the stories of couples that have been-there-and-done-that may inspire you and show you that, yes, it can be done. And you have already paved the path for someone else. That feels good, doesn't it?

IF YOU DON'T

So, your Starter Marriage didn't last. Maybe you are disappointed—after all, didn't you pretty much plan everything down to the littlest detail?—or maybe you're relieved. Either way, you should feel proud that you invested that time and energy and focused on what you identified as really mattering to you.

Before you jump back into the mating market, realize that now is the time to explore where there might have been missteps and what you learned about yourself in the process. Because a Starter Marriage by its nature avoids the drama that typically goes along with a marital dissolution, you and your former spouse will more likely be able to amicably sit down and compare notes about what worked and what didn't.

To truly make a Starter Marriage a success, you should walk away (or stay) with a better understanding of yourself, marriage, commitment, communication, sharing goals and values, and accepting change. You may or may not want to tie the knot again, but you will have a self-awareness that will help you in any relationship, intimate or not.

WHAT'S GOOD ABOUT A STARTER MARRIAGE

- A Starter Marriage allows you and your partner to experience the role of "husband" and "wife."

- In agreeing to the terms of the marital contract, you and your partner will not be able to avoid discussing and agreeing to all potentially sticky issues, including finances, household chores, children—among the topics many couples argue about—and other issues. A marital contract means you and your partner will not be able to avoid the hard conversations, sorry!

- Your marriage won't likely have unrealistic expectations and hidden agendas.

- It may highlight areas in which you are incompatible but were unaware of; you definitely want to be aware of them before you add children to the mix.

- The marital contract holds you and your partner accountable for whatever terms you agreed to in setting up the contract; it's a state-enforceable way of making sure you are both doing what you said you would.

- It will help clarify your own limitations and illuminate areas you might want to work on, either on your own or with help, like with a therapist.

- If you and/or your partner choose not to renew the contract, splitting property, finances, etc., will already be agreed upon, allowing for a quicker and cheaper marital dissolution.

- If you and/or your partner choose not to renew the contract, you will have gained valuable knowledge of what marriage is "really like" (and what you are really like in it), which can help you in future relationships.

- If you and your partner renew the contract, you're willingly choosing to stay married to each other; at this point, you'll need to renegotiate the terms of the contract, which may include other marital models we outline, such as a Parenting Marriage or an Open Marriage.

- Whether you and your partner renew the contract or not, you will be able to celebrate a partnership that was a success by your definition.

WHAT'S NOT SO GOOD ABOUT A STARTER MARRIAGE

• Your partner may not want to renew the marital contract, or you may want out and he/she doesn't (but that is an option in all marriages, Starter or not).

• You'll have the expense of a wedding and honeymoon, and all the related costs.

• You'll have to consult with attorneys to help draft the marital contract before even saying, "I do"—we know, it's not all that romantic.

• You may be subject to feelings and judgments from yourself and others about having a "failed" marriage.

• You may feel judgment from others for not marrying for the "right" reasons.

• You may have to wrestle with feelings of whether you're fully committing yourself or not.

• Embracing a new way of practicing marriage may cause a lot of cognitive dissonance, when you're beliefs and actions don't align.

• You may feel stigma if you don't renew your vows.

• If you accidently get pregnant, you will have to renegotiate the contract.

HOW TO MAKE A STARTER MARRIAGE WORK

• You really want to be married instead of cohabiting.

• You don't measure success by longevity alone.

• You don't feel paralyzed by deadlines.

• You don't see a marriage that ends as a failed marriage.

• You're not marrying with hidden agendas.

• You are interested in understanding and working on your own behaviors, beliefs, and patterns.

• You are committed to giving your all while at the same time understanding that life is uncertain and there are no guarantees.

• You don't idealize or romanticize marriage and expect marriage alone to make you happier, better, or more complete.

- You are okay with gently ignoring or responding to how others perceive your marriage.

- You value commitment.

IS A STARTER MARRIAGE RIGHT FOR ME?

Wondering if you're cut out for a Starter Marriage? Here are a few questions you might want to ask yourself:

- What are my reasons for marrying?

- Why do I want to get married instead of living together?

- Is living together the same as marriage?

- Am I comfortable with the idea of marriage not lasting forever?

- Am I comfortable seeing marriage as a legal contract with a potential end date?

- Am I able to talk openly with my partner about tough issues and sign a document that will hold me accountable for my actions?

- Will I be able to fully commit myself to a marriage if I enter into it with a potential "out" date?

- Do I believe my partner is able to fully commit to a marriage if he or she enters into it with a potential "out" date?

- What do I really think about divorce?

- How does my experience of divorce (through a parent's, a relative's, or a friend's divorce) influence me?

- Is a marriage that ends a "failed" marriage?

- Do I want to have children one day, and will having a Starter Marriage interfere with those plans?

- How would I feel if my partner didn't want to renew the contract but I did?

- How would I feel if I didn't want to renew the contract but my partner did?

- How open would I be with family and friends about choosing a Starter Marriage?

READ MORE

Curious about how to make this marital model work? Here are some books to read for insight and guidance:

- *How To Get Divorced By 30: My Misguided Attempt at a Starter Marriage* by Sascha Rothchild (Plume, 2010).
- *The Mini Marriage: 5 Bite Sized Memoirs of Young Divorce* by Karen Jerabek (CreateSpace Independent Publishing Platform, 2010).
- *Not Your Mother's Divorce: A Practical, Girlfriend-to-Girlfriend Guide to Surviving the End of a Young Marriage* by Kay Moffett and Sarah Touborg (Harmony, 2003).
- *The Starter Marriage and the Future of Matrimony* by Pamela Paul (Random House Trade Paperbacks, 2003).

STARTER MARRIAGE TAKEAWAYS

- A Starter Marriage is a "trial" marriage, giving spouses a chance to see what marriage is really like.
- A Starter Marriage is a legal, time-limited commitment.
- A Starter Marriage is a first marriage and is generally reserved for younger couples that lack life experience.
- In a Starter Marriage, spouses agree that they will not have children.
- Starter Marriages can be renewed or converted into one of the other types of marriages (such as the Parenting Marriage, if the couple chooses to stay together and start a family).
- A Starter Marriage differs from cohabitation on many levels (different expectations from society; when you're married, you're considered family; there are more responsibilities when you are married).
- Starter Marriages have a natural end so couples that don't want to stay together can go their separate ways without a complicated divorce.

Chapter 4

COMPANIONSHIP MARRIAGE:

YOU'VE GOT A FRIEND

"Our culture has gone so crazy with romance that we
have tossed out the door the whole reality that we are
choosing someone to live with, eat with, rear children with,
pay the bills with, and not just have sex with."
—Comment from a reader on the *Huffington Post*

Marta was married three years before she had a sobering aha moment—she and her husband were bad companions. "I thought [romantic love] was very relevant, but I was in love with the sex and the physique of the person and not with the person himself," the twenty-three-year-old from South Korea told us. "We had nothing in common besides tattoos."

Having a shared interest in tattoos is great, but we never considered it the stuff of successful partnerships, either.

Clearly, you can have a romantic marriage without companionship, even if the prognosis for it lasting is not very good. But what about the reverse? Can you have a marriage based on companionship without the romantic love? Absolutely, and we believe a Companionship Marriage is much more sustaining and sustainable than the one you probably have been taught to look for—a marriage that's all about passion-filled love.

When most people hear that a couple is getting married, everyone assumes that the couple values love above all else because this is how it's "supposed" to be. Except that isn't always what people want most of all. In our survey of several hundred people from across the globe, companionship was the number one reason to tie the knot (64 percent) followed by love at 59 percent. That differs somewhat from a 2010 Pew study, in which 72 percent considered companionship a good reason to marry, after love and commitment.

But whether it's number one or number three, it's pretty evident companionship is an important aspect of marriage. While many people enjoy periods of being single and a certain amount can't see being anything but a lifelong singleton, a lot of other people don't really want to be alone forever, especially as they get older.

Barbara, a sixty-two-year-old widow, married Vince because she was afraid to grow old alone. She wanted to know someone else would be in the house with her, and she wanted some legal assurances of being taken care of financially if he died first. It's not that love was completely absent; it just wasn't her *primary* reason. According to Barbara, Vince, who was a resident at the same assisted living facility, was "as good and decent as any other man out there might be." There were no big sparks, but, at her age, she didn't need the glitz.

Mason had no intention of settling down again after he divorced his third wife, but then he became smitten with Amy, a starving artist. Although he is American, Mason, fifty-seven, grew up in Japan—a culture that keenly emphasizes maintaining awareness of how your actions impact others. He knew he could help Amy be more financially secure so she could pursue her art, and, being in a position to help her out financially, he couldn't just sit back and watch her struggle. "I cared about her, and I was truly concerned that if I didn't support her, she'd end up homeless," he told us. While you may consider his decision too self-sacrificing, he believes it was a small price to pay to help a lovely woman he thought was a talented painter. In return, Mason comes home to a great friend, someone to share his day with, and a pretty comfortable lifestyle. And, since he is a frustrated artist himself, their shared love of art is an extra bonus. He imagined a life in which they would enjoy critiquing her work together as well as discussing the artworks they'd see at the many exhibits and museums they would visit.

When Rebecca died at the age of thirty-five of ovarian cancer, her husband, Jesse, had three young children to take care of by himself. But Rebecca's sister Naira, who never married, was happy to step in as their surrogate mom. It was their shared grief as well as Naira's unconditional willingness to be there for him and the kids that made him fall in love with her in a really different way than he did with Rebecca. He sees Naira much more as a friend than as a romantic partner, but she was the kind of friend he wanted to keep around for a long time. To this day, they have a sweet connection, even though the children are grown and live on their own.

Celine, fifty-two, and Dan, fifty-eight, had been together since 1993 but waited to tie the knot until 2005. The reason? Dan had kids from a previous marriage and Celine—who never wanted the responsibility of being a stepmother to young kids—didn't want to marry Dan until his kids were older and out of the house. As much as she loved Dan, if she had been his wife, it would have been that much more difficult and complicated to leave. Being a child of divorce herself, she didn't want to add to the drama Dan's kids had already been through.

These couples came together not necessarily to make a public statement of love or to grow as a person or to have children together or to have sex while hanging from the chandeliers; they married to keep each other company, to help each other emotionally and financially, and to make life easier. Their marriages are less about romance and more about serving an admittedly utilitarian purpose—being with someone who has their back.

While Celine wasn't keen on becoming a stepparent, many other women and men are. Slightly more than 12 percent of all children living with two adults in the United States are part of a stepfamily, according to a 2009 census study. A Pew report indicates 42 percent of U.S. adults have at least one step-relative. A 60 percent divorce rate for second marriages is telling, especially since many have blended families. But marrying for companionship may make for a more successful blended union. According to psychologist James H. Bray of the Baylor College of Medicine, who has studied and written extensively about stepfamilies, stepfamilies tend to fall into one of three categories—neotraditional, matriarchal, and romantic. Matriarchal families, headed by strong, independent women who marry for a companion, not a co-parent, were almost as successful as neotraditional stepfamilies, which he describes as a "contemporary version of the 1950s white picket fence family: it is close-knit, loving, and works very well for a couple with compatible values." The least successful stepfamilies were the romantics, whose unrealistic expectations of immediate family cohesiveness, marital satisfaction, and obedient children prove impossible to achieve.

When Susan and her husband, Michael, exchanged vows in 2004, they were not quite blending families—just two beloved rescue dogs that had brought them together. They were middle-aged when they wed, neither had been married before, neither had children from previous relationships, and having children was not part of their plans. Unbeknownst to Susan before writing this book, she and her husband were entering into a Companionship Marriage. Although they easily could have continued living as an unmarried couple, they, like many of their friends and people their age, found the idea of being legally married more appealing.

The unconscious nature of their decision hit Susan and Michael when they were having dinner with a colleague who asked them, "Why did you get married?"

"We love each other," Susan replied.

Their colleague pressed on. "But, why did you marry? You don't have to get married just because you love someone."

That's true. Initially, Susan and Michael were perplexed. They had never thought that much about their decision to wed, and no one had asked them before. Like so many of the people we interviewed for this book, Susan and Michael admitted they married because they were in love and "it's just what you do."

When they thought about it more, however, they could see that companionship was a huge part of why they wanted to tie the knot. Why does that matter? Well, the expectations of having a companion don't include the need to stay in an intense "in love" state. In truth, that "in love" state fades anyway, as you probably have seen in marriages—and divorces—of your friends and maybe your parents.

As you mature and life circumstances change, your priorities shift. If we were to create a continuum of what's most important to men and women in relationships throughout their life span, it might look something like this (warning: we are generalizing, and you may have other desired traits not listed here, but you get the idea):

- eighteen to twenty-four: good sex (see note below) and good love, aka the madly-in-love stage
- twenty-five to thirty-five: good potential, aka the career-building stage
- thirty-six to fifty: good partner, good co-parent, aka the homemaking, family-making stage
- fifty-one to eighty: good companion, aka the "you'll still like each other when you're empty nesters and retired" stage
- eighty-one to (we hope) a happy, healthy long life: good caretaker, aka the "I'll drive you to the doctor and make sure you take your meds" stage

  (Note: we're aware some of you would include good sex for all the age groups, so go right ahead . . . and good luck!)

Let's face it; people have different needs at different times, which helps explain why it can be hugely challenging to have a lifelong marriage. That's why many people are multiple marriers. But it's also evident that a good chunk of a romantic relationship—especially later in life—is spent wanting your partner to be a good companion.

What if the companionship part came first?

IS COMPANIONSHIP JUST
ANOTHER WORD FOR SETTLING?

In 2009, journalist Lori Gottlieb wrote an essay, "Marry Him," in the *Atlantic* and, a year later, came out with a well-researched book by the same name that expanded her argument. Gottlieb said that instead of spending time looking for Mr. Right, women who want to marry and have children should adjust their expectations and consider marrying Mr. Good Enough. As she good-humoredly writes:

"Don't worry about passion or intense connection. Don't nix a guy based on his annoying habit of yelling 'Bravo!' in movie theaters. Overlook his halitosis or abysmal sense of aesthetics. Because if you want to have the infrastructure in place to have a family, settling is the way to go. Based on my observations, in fact, settling will probably make you happier in the long run, since many of those who marry with great expectations become more disillusioned with each passing year. (It's hard to maintain that level of *zing* when the conversation morphs into discussions about who's changing the diapers or balancing the checkbook.)"

Gottlieb, a forty-eight-year-old single mom who conceived via a sperm donor a decade earlier, used her own frustrating story of looking for The One as a somewhat cautionary tale, but her article and book ruffled a lot of women's feathers. Actually, it set off quite a firestorm, and numerous blogs and articles attacked her logic and saw her as contributing to single women's angst.

Much of the fracas over her article and book rested on the word "settle," which was unfortunately all too often interpreted as choosing a partner who was "less than" or a plain vanilla bore. But Gottlieb and the experts she interviewed weren't advising women to get hitched to just any Joe Blow. Instead, she advocated that women throw out their quest for finding a soul mate, a man who will "complete" them, and the rom-com fantasy of love and marriage, and instead look for a man who would make a good partner. Not a ho-hum partner, but a good partner.

In that respect, we agree. A Companionship Marriage is not based on marrying someone who will be your "everything." It's not based on marrying someone who is going to be the best lover and provider, homemaker, or father or mother (remember, not all people want kids or have kids. If you want kids, please take a look at the Parenting Marriage chapter). Honestly, you are not going to be someone else's everything either, even if your mother thinks you are perfect and even if you believe you're perfect, too. We hate to break it to you, but you're not perfect—but you will be a good enough person for someone, or maybe several someones. That's a good thing.

Would some say you'd be settling or lowering the bar to marry for companionship instead of love? Sure. But because people want different things from marriage (and want different things from it at different times), anyone who insists you'd be lowering the bar wouldn't be right. "My husband and I married for companionship and compatibility," one couple of fifteen years proudly wrote to us. If that's what they wanted and that's what they have and they're happy, we'd say that's a marriage that works.

Rather than calling it "settling," we prefer to say that by identifying your priorities instead of spending energy and time looking for The One, you are better able to pick a mate who will share those priorities. That's making a marriage successful by your own terms. It isn't a matter of semantics, either; people are happier when their expectations match their reality.

A thirty-five-year-old unmarried Seattle woman who told us that, while she could do without the sexual aspect of marriage, in part because of a history of being sexually abused, she does want a mate one day. "I am not a sexual person. That being said, I want companionship. A lot. I'm a really touchy-feeling person; hugs are awesome and one of the things that keep me sane. When I think about getting married, I feel that saying vows in front of friends and family is important to that companionship for stability. That someone would be willing to say these vows is important to me."

That is *not* lowering the bar or settling.

Another woman contacted us to thank us (as many others have, which confirms for us that there's a great hunger for this discussion). After reading about our proposal to tweak marriage, she told us that she felt validated for the first time about her own marital choice. In the past, she often wondered if her decision to marry for reasons other than romantic love was a mistake. That's the message society keeps sending out. She now realizes that her marriage—one she says is "based on our lifestyles and desires in life"—is no less a happy marriage than one based on romantic love.

Yet another reader admits that, while love was part of the reason she married her husband two years ago, "common interests, political views, companionship, and other various factors carried a lot more weight than love actually did. . . . This may sound harsh to some, but I can honestly say that I don't love my husband the way I used to, but there are other things that help keep me invested in our marriage."

She, like the others, sought someone she could share interests and friendship with. One definition of companionship is "the good feeling that comes from being with someone else," and that's actually a pretty grand feeling. Companionship is the stuff you fall back on when physical attraction and appearance fade (as they inevitably do), as comfortable as your favorite pair of worn jeans or T-shirt. So if people are willing to accept companionship later on in life, what's wrong with putting it at the top of your list? Sure, it may be nowhere near as sexy or exciting as romantic love, but it's just as valid a reason to say, "I do."

We love how one woman explains the success of her long marriage: "I've been married to at least ten different men. They just all happen to be the same one. The secret of our fifty-seven-year marriage is that we are totally supportive of the other's continual transformation, glad to accept the anxiety that accompanies that freedom instead of the boredom that drives most people apart." She beautifully captures the sobering reality that relationships aren't static, nor should the people in them be.

In one of our surveys, we asked people around the world about the role of romantic love versus utilitarian love in marriage. The results were about fifty-fifty. In other words, people thought both had value. What mattered more to them, we discovered, is that the type of love a person used to guide his or her decision on choosing a mate was less important than if that decision was in line with his or her values about love.

This is not unlike how some people view their livelihood. To many, their job is nothing more than a means to an end. They don't have to feel passionate about it, and the trade-off is that they have a steady paycheck that affords them a satisfying life in their days and hours off. If and when this is congruent with their belief system about work, they have relatively few complaints about their job.

Insert someone else into that same job who needs to be passionate about his work, and he will be pretty miserable if he doesn't feel jazzed to go to work every day. For many people who took our survey, staying with a mate who is good enough is not a problem; they are content with their choice. But we would be remiss if we didn't acknowledge that some people have big regrets that they chose companionship as their focus over love. For those people, there's a lingering nagging doubt that they've missed out on a grand passion by letting The One get away or by not waiting long enough to find him or her.

One woman lamented to us, "He never had a sex drive that matched mine. Any mutual passion we had is pretty much gone after twenty-plus years. I don't want anyone else to take care of that part of my life, but I sure wish he was more interested and enthusiastic."

And one man professed, "I married a woman who had the qualities I was looking for in a wife. I avoided the love thing because I had been hurt badly, and I was determined to never let love derail my life again. After twenty-five years, I can say, my decision was practical, wise, and wholly unfulfilling. I know I have to face the fact that I will never know what it is like to be with someone I am madly in love with. Yes, love may fade with time, but so do the practical reasons for being married in the first place. So go ahead and find someone you love—it may not work out, but I can guarantee that you won't regret it while it lasts."

Does he make a good point? Yes, although he is somewhat contradictory in his feelings about how love derailed his life while "guaranteeing" there will be no regrets if you allow love to derail your own life. The problem with his thinking, however, and the problem most people face when searching for a mate, is that he may never actually meet someone he's "madly in love with." He may, but he may not. Ever. After all, there are no guarantees in life or love. So to project how much happier he might be in some imagined relationship he believes he's missing out on is an illusion; people are really bad predictors of how happy they'll be in the future or in certain circumstances because that happiness is based on how they feel right now, according to Harvard psychologist and *Stumbling on Happiness* author Daniel Gilbert. So instead of regretting that he didn't marry for love, he might instead end up regretting that he didn't marry a good gal when he had the chance to.

Couples that consider themselves good friends tend to be quite harmonious, handle conflict in a healthy and respectful way, and share similar goals and values on the big-picture stuff, like raising kids and religion, sociologist Paul Amato has found.

That doesn't sound so bad (again, you can skip the kids if you'd prefer to be childfree). It certainly doesn't sound like settling to us.

"Love will make you blind to the other person's faults. When you go into a marriage with your eyes open, it will make life a lot easier," a Southern California woman in an arranged marriage of eight years wrote us. She agreed, at first reluctantly, to have her parents find her a mate because she was ready to have a family, she was looking for security, and she frankly admits, "I wasn't getting any younger."

She does not regret her decision.

"Love will come when you see your partner take care of you, your kids, your family, and when they respect you and when they do the small, little everyday things that matter. Love develops when you have mutual respect for one another," she wrote us. "But romantic love can disappear when the hardships of life take over. Romantic love is usually a changing emotion. But when you go into a marriage that is practical, love will develop. . . . I wish we didn't have fantasy ideas of marriage. Because when we do, it's a big reality check after marriage."

This seems like a good place to pause and make clear that we are in no way encouraging or endorsing you to pick or stay with a partner who, despite sharing your values and goals, has other traits, attitudes, or behaviors that are damaging to you or the relationship. Being with a good enough partner is not the same as being a martyr.

SHOULD YOU MARRY YOUR BFF?

What we found from our survey is that people who were happy with their marriage—regardless of whether it was based on idealized love or practical love—believed it was because they chose the right type of marriage for their situation.

One couple in their thirties who'd been together for eight years told us, "We were in the military when we got married. Still going strong with a three-year-old now. Now I'm a cop in Boston and she's a nurse. I think it works 'cause we've never had that 'romantic love.' Always been more of a friendship with awesome sex."

Companionship, yes. Friendship, yes. Best friend? Maybe not. While we're all for you picking a spouse you genuinely like, marrying someone you consider your best friend is dicey. It's yet another instance of trying to have a mate meet all your emotional and physical needs. Generally, all that does is lead to frustration (and typically, people are much more tolerant and accepting of a best friend's bad behavior than a spouse's).

In her work, Susan has seen many women disappointed that they can't talk to their husbands about the details of their day the same way they do with girlfriends who relish the same information. And she's seen lots of men who resent being bombarded with information they can't process (or maybe don't want to). Call it a male brain–female brain thing or a Mars-Venus thing, but we'll bet most heteros have experienced this with at least one romantic partner in their lifetime.

This begs the question, should mates be best friends? No, says Karen, who was in a lesbian marriage for five years. She told us that in her experience, "it's dangerous to have a spouse as a best friend because if problems develop, you don't have a neutral person to talk to." That was knowledge she really would have valued when she and her wife were having difficulties. "You've got to have that objective feedback that you can only get from an outside friend," she says. She blames their extra-close relationship as contributing to their downfall. Ironically, they have remained best friends since their divorce, but they just can't be in a romantic relationship together. Combining the two didn't work.

So forget the fantasy partner and forget the best friend. Being good companions means you're pretty focused on what you do well together, and, honestly, few people do *everything* well together.

CHILDFREE COMPANIONSHIP

Perhaps no one understands the desire for companionship in a marriage more than couples that choose to be childfree (and we are making a distinction between childfree couples that don't want kids and childless couples that want kids but for a variety of reasons are unable to have them). Raising a family is a huge reason why many couples wed. But why marry if you don't plan to have children?

"Love and companionship" is what Laura S. Scott found herself saying to the many people who asked her that. But she isn't alone. The author of *Two Is Enough: A Couple's Guide to Living Childless by Choice* found that companionship was considered a priority by many of the couples she surveyed for her Childless by Choice Project.

So did Amy Blackstone, a sociology professor at the University of Maine, who surveyed childfree couples about how they go about creating a family when clearly there are no children involved. Marriage was what made them see themselves as a family, and companionship was often mentioned as a motivating factor to tie the knot.

"I thought my husband would be a great friend and dependable companion through my life," one woman in our survey told us. "I wasn't keen on having children back then, so procreation didn't factor into my plans."

And we'll leave you with what a wise thirty-year-old bride-to-be told us. "I am currently engaged, and logic played a huge role in my decision. Not love or lust. I love my fiancé, but it's because of our shared values and acceptances of differences, not because of a mushy nebulous feeling. I've done that feeling before . . . and it ends in a mess.

"I'm marrying my fiancé because he lets me be who I really am. We both don't want kids; we both want the same life. We are equally educated, rational, and are making this choice together because it makes sense, not because some emotion is telling me this is what I should be doing."

BECOMING COMPANIONS IF YOU'RE ALREADY MARRIED

As you saw above, most marriages drift into Companionship Marriages at some point or another, often after the kids leave. That doesn't mean, however, that you can't shape the way that companionship looks.

Consider Warren and Betsy Talbot. The forty-four-year-olds were friends first and married—a second marriage for both—for the tax perks they'd get instead of continuing to live together. The childfree couple made tons of money in their corporate careers, had a huge house that they filled with what they now describe as "a lot of crap," and were considered by many to have it all—big jobs, big house, big lives. But, in the first couple of years together, they were drifting apart. They were focused on consumption, not each other. They admitted to us they were headed for divorce if for no other reason than they had lost meaningful connection with each other. If you've been married for any length of time, does that sound familiar?

After the sudden life-threatening health issues of two loved ones, they came to the realization that, yes, life is short. What were they doing with their life? Just because they were childfree didn't mean that they were truly free. When they examined their choices, they saw they were chained to their careers, home, and possessions. They decided to make their relationship a priority, and they set out to create the life they really wanted. What they longed for was to be travel companions. So with a clear vision and a shared goal, they sold everything and have been traveling around the globe since 2010 and writing about their adventures online at Married With Luggage and in books.

They admitted to us that it's hard to live so unconventionally. Not having children and not making other family members a priority was a double strike against them. But they have re-created a marriage that started off for financial reasons and turned into one based on fun and companionship. And one that keeps evolving.

"We came upon the idea of treating our relationship more like a performance contract between partners, one where you can choose to renew, renegotiate, or cancel on an annual basis. We weren't sure if we were brilliant or insane," Betsey Talbot writes.

They continue to reinvent their marriage every year on their anniversary, when they review all that's happened in the past twelve months, personally and as a couple. Then they take turns talking about what they'd like to see get better, after some hugs for reassurance. Finally, they ask each other if they want to renew—which each has so far—and then agree out loud to the changes they are going to make and why.

"Anytime you're willing to enter into negotiation it means you find value in the relationship. And knowing we have a yearly renewal keeps us both on our toes. There is nothing more frustrating than exchanging vows and then forgetting them. This is an ongoing enterprise, and we want to keep it sustainable," she says.

"Most people think the best thing we've ever done is to travel the world. But we'll tell you without a doubt that the best thing we've ever done is create a partnership so strong we think we can do anything together," they state on their website.

It's hard to argue with that.

KEEP THE MARRIAGE, CHANGE THE RULES

Michelle consciously made the decision to marry her husband, Craig, fifteen years ago because they were great companions if not sexual partners. "We are compatible in so many ways it feels wasteful to throw out our marriage because we don't work sexually. We still love each other, enjoy each other's company, and co-parent beautifully. We like our life together," she wrote us.

After the frenetic early years of childrearing, when few couples are having much sex anyway, Michelle was suddenly struck by how much she missed passion. She and her husband are bravely exploring an Open Marriage, which she talks about so candidly in Chapter 9.

What the Talbots and Michelle and Craig have done is renegotiate the terms of their marital contract—they started off one way and rather than divorce, they turned their marriage into something else. Their stories are a valuable lesson for anyone who regrets marrying for companionship versus romantic love. If your marriage isn't working, do something different. Change your attitude, change your behavior, change your actions, switch to one of the other marital models we offer in this book. After all, half of the success (or not) of your marriage is in your hands.

WHAT'S GOOD ABOUT A COMPANIONSHIP MARRIAGE

- It's easier finding someone who meets your needs for companionship than someone you consider The One.

- Utilitarian love is less fragile than romantic love, which tends to fade early in a marriage.

- Your marriage will be based on common goals and, if you choose, interests.

- It offers a good foundation for connection if you don't plan to have children.

- Relationships tend to become companionate in the later years anyway.

- Your marriage will be focused on what you and your spouse do well together.

- Expectations of your marriage and spouse may be more realistic, so there's less of a chance of being disappointed and frustrated.

- There's no ambiguity about what's expected.

- It offers a different way to experience intimacy.

- It's less tumultuous than a marriage based on romantic love.

- Friendship offers a solid foundation for a partnership.

- Marrying a good companion may be better than being alone.

- You will have a partner aligned with your values.

- You will have a partner to do things with.

- You will have someone to help with caregiving, especially if you're older.

- You will have someone to support you emotionally, if not necessarily financially.

- You will be a couple in a coupled world.

- You will have a partner with whom you can share personal growth.

WHAT'S NOT SO GOOD ABOUT
A COMPANIONSHIP MARRIAGE

- It may feel like settling.
- You may face judgment and misunderstanding from others.
- You may feel something is missing in your love life.
- You might get bored more easily or quickly.
- You may become unhappy with your choice.
- You may be sexually tempted.
- You may be jealous of others who appear to have passionate love.
- You may feel resentment that you didn't get what you really wanted.
- You may get frustrated with your partner for not being able to give you more.
- You may have a lingering sense of self-doubt.
- You may have to work harder to create your own happiness.

HOW TO MAKE A COMPANIONSHIP MARRIAGE WORK

This marriage is probably one of the easier marriages to design (whether you are going into a marriage or redefining your existing matrimony) because it is based on the simple concept of friendship. Of course, couples can always incorporate passionate love into this marriage, but the primary reason for having a Companionship Marriage is to have a mate who is a really good friend; a really good partner for work, travel, and fun; and someone who will keep you from being alone.

Here are the qualities or attitudes we think you'd need to possess in order to have this marriage be successful:

- You are not a hopeless romantic at heart.
- You don't believe one person can or should fulfill all your needs.
- You are emotionally secure.
- You have good self-esteem.

- You are goal-oriented.
- You believe the day-to-day activities of life are easier if shared.
- You are willing to work things through with each other. Friendship matters to you, and you know how to be a good friend.
- You don't have a strong need for sexual passion.
- You and your partner are compatible in many ways.
- You value stability over risk.
- You accept people as they are.
- You are comfortable having your spouse be the extent of your family and having your relationship be the main focus of your life.
- You are more comfortable as part of a couple than as a single.
- You both want to get married, but you don't have to get married.
- You make a conscious choice to be companions rather than companions by default.
- You agree to continue to work on your primary relationship and not take the other for granted.
- You are satisfied with having a sweet, easy love for your partner and you don't have to feel "in love."
- You're not a perfectionist, and you don't expect your spouse to meet all of your needs and wants.
- You have goals and interests that you already share with your mate or want to share with a mate.

IS A COMPANIONSHIP MARRIAGE RIGHT FOR ME?

Wondering if you're cut out for a Companionship Marriage? Here are a few questions you might want to ask yourself:

- What does companionship mean to me?
- What about having a Companionship Marriage excites me?
- What scares me?

- What would I gain?
- What would I miss?
- What qualities make a good companion?
- Am I a romantic at heart?
- How important is romantic love to me?
- How important is friendship in a marriage to me?
- Should I marry my best friend?
- How do I feel about the word "settling" as it relates to relationships?
- What would I want to accomplish in a Companionship Marriage that I couldn't have in any other marital model?
- Would I be sexually tempted by others?
- How would I manage those temptations?
- Do I believe it's okay for people to marry so they're not alone?

READ MORE

Curious about how to make this marital model work? Here are some books to read for insight and guidance:

- *The Business of Love: 9 Best Practices for Improving the Bottom Line of Your Relationship* by John Curtis (IOD Press, 2006).
- *First Comes Marriage: Modern Relationship Advice from the Wisdom of Arranged Marriages* by Reva Seth (Touchstone, 2008).
- *Marry Him: The Case for Settling for Mr. Good Enough* by Lori Gottlieb (Dutton Adult, 2010).
- *The Seven Principles for Making Marriage Work: A Practical Guide from the Country's Foremost Relationship Expert* by John Gottman and Nan Scott (Crown, 1999).
- *Two Is Enough: A Couple's Guide to Living Childless by Choice* by Laura Scott (Seal Press, 2009).
- *Why We Love: The Nature and Chemistry of Romantic Love* by Helen Fisher (Holt Paperbacks, 2004).

COMPANIONSHIP MARRIAGE TAKEAWAYS

- A Companionship Marriage is less about passion-filled romantic love and more about practical love.

- A Companionship Marriage is one in which your mate is a friend and someone to do things with.

- A Companionship Marriage is not centered around having children. Some couples are childfree by choice, others have grown children who are out of the house when they marry.

- A Companionship Marriage is an attractive alternative for people who do not want to grow old alone.

- The standard for a Companionship Marriage is that your spouse is "good enough."

- Companionship is the basis of all good marriages.

- A Companionship Marriage is often what empty-nesters create once their parenting role reverts back to their mate role.

Chapter 5

PARENTING MARRIAGE:

TRULY PLANNED PARENTHOOD

"I take a practical view of raising children. I put a sign in
their rooms—checkout time is eighteen years."

—Erma Bombeck

*W*hen Ryan and Lisa married, love had nothing to do with it.
It's not that the two San Francisco Bay Area residents in their
early thirties weren't in love—they were. But the reason they stood
before friends and family and said, "I do," was because, after living
together for seven years, they decided they wanted to have children.

No one at the wedding reception knew that, nor did anyone
know why the couple hadn't vowed to be together "until death do us
part." That's because they'd privately agreed to stay together until
their last child was off to college, some eighteen to twenty years from
now. They may still be together after that, Ryan says, but neither he
nor his new bride is promising that to the other.

On the surface, Ryan and Lisa's marriage looks like any other
young couple's, a traditional marriage. Except it is not; they are bending
the institution to fit what they want from marriage—which is to co-parent. Sadly, they are unable to express that openly for fear of judgment.

Ryan and Lisa have taken a different approach than many couples. Instead of marrying with the expectation that they will put each other first, they tied the knot knowing that they are putting their future children first. This runs counter to what some marital experts advise, which is that you need to romance and date your spouse because, once the kids go off to college, it will be just the two of you again. If you haven't been keeping the marital flames alive, you may be disconnected and likely headed for divorce. But here's a secret few people know unless they've been in a long-term marriage with children—very few couples actually continually romance and date each other. Most parents put their kids first, not their spouse. Or, a spouse gets displaced in favor of the kids. Either way, it becomes a huge source of bad feelings between spouses. If this is what the majority of parents are doing anyway, shouldn't you marry someone who will be the best possible parent, not necessarily the best romantic or lifelong partner?

That's where the Parenting Marriage comes in. A Parenting Marriage unites two people who want to have children and who commit to stay together until they launch the last child to adulthood. The goal is to provide a stable and loving home for children to thrive. As most couples will readily admit, once you throw kids into the mix, everything changes. Because this marital model is less about love for your mate and more about commitment to raising a child or children, it has the most requirements and prerequisites, giving new meaning to the phrase "planned parenthood."

WHAT'S LOVE GOT TO DO WITH PARENTING?

Before we explain to you the intricacies of such a marriage, you may be wondering, what about love? Don't kids need their parents to love each other? How else will they learn about what makes for a successful marriage? Those are good and important questions.

Parents do not need to be married to successfully co-parent and raise healthy, happy kids. Prior to states legalizing same-sex marriage, gay and lesbian parents had long been raising children together successfully. And parents don't necessarily need to love each other either—just look at the many divorced couples that have managed to be better co-parents to their children than husbands or wives to each other.

And there are studies that back this up. Penn State sociologist Paul Amato researched whether married parents provided more to their children than unmarried parents. What he found was hardly surprising; children do best cognitively, emotionally, and socially in childhood through adulthood when they have two parents who get along, are involved in their kids' lives, and live under the same roof. Children also do well when their parents have an amicable relationship but live apart, either because they are separated, divorced, or never married, as long as they can maintain regular contact with both parents.

Kids do the worst when their parents live apart, have a contentious relationship, and when one parent—often the father—doesn't participate in their lives. But here's where the case for marriage falls apart: If children live with married parents who have a high-conflict relationship, they have almost as many problems as kids whose parents are divorced and fighting. What kids need, Amato says, is a "good enough marriage"—a relationship in which the parents get along for the most part and work as a team to provide enough of the things kids need in order to function well.

Sociologist Kathleen Gerson found similar results while researching her 2010 book, *The Unfinished Revolution: How a Generation Is Reshaping Family, Work, and Gender in America*. While some kids who grew up in a single-parent home told her they wished their divorced parents had stayed together, four out of ten thought their life might have been better if their parents had split. That's a lot of kids who were aware of their parents' unhappiness.

Here's the humbling truth: Children don't care all that much if their parents are fulfilled in their marriage. They don't care if their parents are married, and, for the most part, they don't care who stays home with them, Dad or Mom. What kids want and need more than anything is stability, consistency, and a close relationship with their parents. When they have that, they do well regardless of whether they have one, two, or four parents, and whether those parents are straight or gay, married or unmarried, biological, adoptive, or step-parents. Many years of research have proved that the way a child adjusts to life's many challenges can be helped or impeded by the quality of a marriage and co-parenting relationships.

Given how fundamental kids' needs for stability and closeness are, it should be easy to accommodate them, right? Healthy relationships do that easily. But, when a relationship goes south—or when it isn't good from the get-go—a child might feel like he or she is living in a combat zone in a war that never ends. Emotional chaos and relational destruction are just some of the fallout of these unhealthy dynamics.

Anthropologist Sarah Blaffer Hrdy goes a step further in busting the two-parent model when she points out that there may even be other family configurations that are just as beneficial to a child's welfare, such as alloparenting, which is when adults help care for someone else's child. "To say that a married mother with children is actually better off than a single mother with just one person taking care of the kids, well, duh, that's obvious. But we don't know, for example, that those children are better off than they would be if they were in a family with a mother and a father and a grandmother and nieces and nephews in the family, or if they were better off with a grandmother, an aunt, and a mother," she notes. "We really don't know because those aren't the kinds of studies we've done. The studies have all looked at married versus unmarried or nuclear family versus single mother."

In some ways, parents who place their children in the hands of daycare centers, baby-sitting co-ops, grandparents, preschools, and nannies are creating mini-alloparenting arrangements. So, too, are the many same-sex couples that create complex extended families in their desire to become parents, as Judith Stacey details in her book *Unhitched: Love, Marriage, and Family Values from West Hollywood to Western China.*

According to Stacey, gay men who have children together are the most stable families of all she's encountered in her many years of studying alternative families. "For men to become parents without women is very difficult," she observes. "Only a small percentage are willing and able to make the commitment." That commitment and determination to become a parent may be essential to raise children with the stability they need. If, as she says, some gay men can "willingly unhitch their sexual and romantic desires from their domestic ones in order to become parents," perhaps it's time that hetero couples follow their lead.

NOT NEW, BUT GROWING

In some ways, heteros already have started to choose parenting over romantic love. Along with the gazillion dating sites based on mutual interests, there now are a number of co-parenting sites where singles can "shop" for a co-parent—not necessarily The One, not even one who is "good enough," but one that will just be an equal parenting partner, no wedding vows required. And despite the fact that this new trend doesn't require marriage (although some co-parents choose to marry), it's a great example of how people are unapologetically creating families outside the traditional norms.

Modamily.com was the first such site in the United States when it launched in 2012. Other sites such as Coparenting.com, Coparentingmatch.com, and Pollentree.com have also popped up around the globe. Rather than go to an adoption agency or sperm bank, unmarried people, gay or straight, who want a child can find a co-parenting partner based on such things as shared values and interests. Often the co-parents live in the same home and run the household together as if they were married, but not always. The arrangements, according to Modamily founder and chief executive officer Ivan Fatovic, require legal assistance for a co-parenting agreement, which includes who pays for what; custody arrangements, etc.; and background checks.

While it may be hard to wrap your head around such an odd arrangement, just consider how people meet potential mates nowadays. Many turn to online dating sites and some fall in love, marry, and have a baby or two with someone they met online. How many singles run a background check on a potential mate? We don't know of any. In this respect, Modamily has it right.

The poster mom for parenting partnerships is undoubtedly Rachel Hope. A real estate developer and freelance writer in Los Angeles, forty-one-year-old Hope is the mother of two children, ages twenty-three and five. In 1990, when Hope was just eighteen, she made a mature decision (although others may say she was too young): "I didn't want to waste time searching for the 'elusive soul mate.' So when my best friend Glenn and I started talking one day about our respective desire for a child, we looked at each other and said, 'Why don't we make a baby together and not marry?'"

Their son Jesse was born a year later, and they have been involved parents ever since, sharing living space most of that time. Hope eagerly described for us how, before she got pregnant, they came to a mutual agreement on everything—from who would pay for what, what kind of education their child should get, and how to handle it if one of them became romantically involved and wanted to bring someone else into the mix.

You can imagine the criticism friends and family had for them. "There's something wrong with you," and, "You just can't commit," were two common themes. Their situation was so far out of the box that it really made people squirm. It's hard to argue with success, however. The two were well matched as co-parents, and Hope says Jesse turned out to be a well-adjusted young man who has never doubted that both of his parents cherish him. And as one TV talk show host joked as she described her odd-but-conflict-free partnership, "Wow, an added benefit. Because you're not married, you don't hate each other."

And that was true. The first birth was so successful that Hope decided to do it again, this time with another platonic friend—Jesse's godfather, Paul. Together, they had Grace. Hope believes that this type of childrearing is about as close to tribal living as you can get in the modern world, and she strongly believes that it is the ideal model for childrearing. She hopes her story and her book, *Family By Choice: Platonic Partnered Parenting,* will give others who have the same desire to be a parent but who don't have a partner, permission to make their dream a reality as well.

She is now on her third quest for a baby-daddy, with no need to have a romantic connection with him, just like with the previous two fathers. She says that she's seeking a man who lives near her, is healthy and fit, and "has his financial stuff together."

Is it a positive or negative trend? It's probably too soon to know, but there are many other cultures around the world that have made raising children their number one purpose in life, and they do just fine. And while many in Western cultures say they value raising children, marriages based on love and romance often don't fare as well, as you're about to see. In any event, the thought and planning that goes into these kinds of co-parenting arrangements should be an inspiration and a model that all couples that want to have kids should follow.

THE PROBLEM WITH LOVE-BASED PARENTING

See if this sounds familiar: Two people date, fall madly in love, maybe move in together, agree to wed, and then vow before family and friends to be together "until death do us part." Often, the couple has talked about having children—how many, when to start a family, what religion the child will be raised in, who will stay home, etc., all essential discussions.

Then baby arrives. More often than not, one of the parents has a closer connection to the baby, usually the mom in hetero marriages, and the less-involved parent begins to feel marginalized, unappreciated, and neglected. All the attention is now being diverted somewhere else; the special moments the couple used to share now revolve around the baby—the latest cute thing she did or he said—and a once-active sex life fades into the background (except, perhaps, for the purposes of creating more little beings who will also interfere with the marriage). It's not everyone's experience, but, according to relationship expert John Gottman, marital satisfaction plummets in the first year or so after the birth of a baby for about 67 percent of new parents.

Now, the couple takes on a new level of relating—or unrelating, as the case may be. Raising children can be challenging; living 24/7 with a spouse can be challenging; doing both is most definitely challenging.

Dashed expectations, exhaustion, infrequent sex, and a general "What about *me*?" feeling more often than not become the foundation of the marriage—at least until the kids are older and on their own.

The product of a couple's mutual love becomes the cause of their mutual discord. Many couples find it impossible to reconnect as husband and wife after kids come on the scene. For some, the sense of disconnect can even happen before the kids arrive if they're struggling with fertility issues. While some eventually end up divorced, a certain percentage stays—and often suffers—"for the kids." Despite their best efforts to lead happy fulfilled lives while providing a sturdy foundation for children, they seem to have gotten the opposite result.

The problem isn't whether or not couples have the best intentions when they tie the knot—don't most of us have the best intentions when we're committing to be with someone? But if people really want to provide the stability that children need to thrive, a vow— which is really a vague promise—to make it forever just isn't enough. You need to pick a partner who will be the best person to co-parent with you—not the "love of your life" or your soul mate—and thoroughly detail and agree to how your child will be raised. We go into more depth in our prenup section, but among the details we urge would-be co-parents to consider are the following:

- Infertility issues (Are you prepared, emotionally and financially, for IVF? How many treatments? Would you adopt?)
- How and where do you plan to raise your child?
- How many children would you like to have, and how far apart in age?
- Do you want your kids to be circumcised (if appropriate)?
- Will you vaccinate your kids?
- What if you have a special-needs child?
- Do you want your kids to go to public schools or private schools?
- Who will stay home with the kids, if anyone?
- How will you handle differences in parenting styles? (i.e., How will you discipline? Will you raise your kids with a certain religion?)

- Who else will be involved in childcare?
- How will childcare duties be split?
- How much do you plan to save for college?

It's exhausting just to think about that, and we haven't even covered all the nuances of parenting and co-parenting. So why not just agree to have kids and make up the rules as you go along, the way your parents did and their parents did? As tempting—and seemingly easier—as that may be, please know that if you end up divorcing, you will be forced to figure this out anyway, plus you'll most likely be paying attorneys and mediators a lot of money if you can't agree to a co-parenting plan yourselves. And even if you don't divorce, these are the issues that many couples consistently argue about, leading to all sorts of stress, frustrations, resentments, and disappointments. In other words, there's no way to get around facing the realities of parenting; doesn't it make more sense to talk about it—and prepare as best you can—*before* you become pregnant or adopt?

We think so.

Of course, you are not going to be able to anticipate each and every possible situation because people lose or change jobs, relocate, decide to go back to school for advanced degrees, become sick or disabled, or even die. Life is not a straight and narrow path. But it's so much easier to make those changes when you have a strong foundation in place for creating a family as you've envisioned it.

THERE'S A BENEFIT TO BEING KID-CENTRIC

Just as marriage has changed throughout history, so, too, has the treatment of children within marriage. In early Rome, babies could be left for dead by parents—without penalty or social stigma—for many reasons, including the presence of physical deformities, family poverty, parental conflict, or just for being one of too many children. A lucky son or daughter might be passed along to friends, but, more often than not, he or she was abandoned.

Sometimes, children became young slaves, meaning that others

treated them as pets and "kept [them] around the house for play purposes. Some of these children were genuinely loved and educated . . .
but more often than not, they were simply for jester-like entertainment or pedophilic gratification." In the Middle Ages, some parents
indentured their children to domestic service, exchanging them "for
four to six sheep, and twelve livres in cash." One year in 1900s New
York, the local chapter of the Society for the Prevention of Cruelty to
Children took in about 15,000 children, "in many cases cruelty on
the part of their own parents, in others on the part of those in whose
custody the children have been left by parents unwilling or incompetent to take care of them."

Obviously, most countries have come a long way since then, and
children now have many more rights and protections. Still, millions
of children are abused and neglected yearly—overwhelmingly at the
hands of their biological parents. However, fewer children experience either if they live with their married biological parents.

In fact, children who grow up in families with both their biological parents in a low-conflict marriage are better off in a number
of ways than children who grow up in single-, step-, or cohabiting-
parent households, according to research by the Center for Law and
Social Policy. As Sara McLanahan of Princeton University, one of the
world's leading scholars on how family form impacts child well-being,
says, if society were to design a system from scratch to ensure that a
child's basic needs would be met, it would look remarkably similar to
the two-parent family. In theory, it would offer children access to the
time and financial resources of two adults and provide "a system of
checks and balances that promote quality parenting."

That is indeed the theory behind the mom-dad-kids model. In
reality, however, raising children in an environment of disappointments, resentments, conflict, power struggles, dashed dreams,
unmet needs, boredom, and unrealistic expectations—and who
hasn't seen at least some of those behaviors in a marriage?—may not
be the healthiest model.

What if you take away the romantic aspect of the parent's
relationship—or at least make it less important? What if instead of

romance, you have a good working relationship with your mate but make raising happy, healthy kids your main focus? We have not read or heard of one study that indicated that parents must be in love with each other to parent successfully, and we've seen plenty of evidence that couples either divorce or stay miserably in a marriage "for the kids' sake" when they are no longer in love with each other. That is why we are proposing the Parenting Marriage. There is too much at stake to let love alone guide quality parenting.

TAKING MARRIAGE DOWN FROM THE PEDESTAL

A Parenting Marriage sounds good on paper, but what can you really expect from this kind of nuptial arrangement? As a relatively new concept, there are some unanswered questions, yet it's clear that a Parenting Marriage addresses some of the major flaws of other family lifestyle options. Ryan and Lisa, the Bay Area couple that recently embarked on a Parenting Marriage, are, like any other couple, finding their way as they go along.

One thing they share with others in a Parenting Marriage or partnership is the feeling that they are doing something taboo; they are wary to talk about their choices openly for fear of being looked down on or judged. That wasn't a problem for fifty-one-year-old Los Angeles therapist Rami Aizic, although his parents couldn't understand why he was planning to have a baby with a woman he'd met through a mutual friend. They weren't married, they were never going to get married, they weren't living together nor would they, and they weren't even in love. Aizic is gay, and he always wanted a child. He was going to adopt until he took an adoption counselor's words to heart—rather than convince himself that he wanted a child so much that he'd take any child, such as one with disabilities or a different ethnicity, he should be honest about what he truly wanted. That sealed his decision. "I wanted something that really came from me."

He and his co-parenting partner, who is straight, spent months getting to know each other and their parenting philosophies. They also went to a couples therapist and a family therapist. Aizic believed he'd met the perfect woman to be the mother of his child. "She was definitely someone that I trusted and I liked. I liked her sensibility, I liked her sensitivity, I liked her style, I liked her demeanor. In terms of parenting, I knew from early on that she would be a very good mother," he says.

They didn't write down a formal agreement defining who would be responsible for what, but they agreed to share expenses and time fifty-fifty with their daughter, Bailey, until she was old enough to have her own ideas. Bailey, now fifteen, was tired of bouncing back and forth between houses and lives full time with her mom. But Aizic is as hands-on as ever. Because their daughter never knew any other arrangement, her parents' unusual arrangement feels natural. They used age-appropriate language to explain why they didn't live together.

Now, Bailey embraces it. "Her personality is very much an activist, as she likes to call herself. She loves that she's got this non-mainstream configuration of a family," Aizic says with a laugh. They are open about their situation—living in a progressive and diverse area helps—and have generally found a welcoming community, although Aizic doesn't doubt that Bailey has experienced some reactions that may have been difficult for her.

And as much as they are good co-parents, there are some negatives to their arrangement. Like most couples, when there are disagreements in a parenting style, someone usually gives in. Aizic admits he has often been the one to do that in recognition of the mother-daughter relationship. Beyond that, because they live separately, "there isn't the ability necessarily to show Bailey how two people work through conflict."

Plus, Aizic has some sadness around not being the parent who's around 24/7. "I think if I had a full-time child, I would feel like she has a much stronger connection to me." Despite that, he has no regrets. They are a family.

Jeannie's entry into co-parenting was radically different than Aizic's. "I married my first husband for love, and it was a nightmare," the middle-aged woman from Canada told us. Her husband was depressed and increasingly became physically and emotionally abusive toward their two girls. Although she didn't want to divorce and didn't believe in it, she felt she had no choice after her husband sent their older daughter to the hospital. She left when they were six months old and two years old, swearing she'd never marry again.

But life was much harder in some ways after the split. The pressure of having to support two young kids and provide them with the care and supervision they needed was next to impossible. She began dating a coworker. "I didn't love him, or even have very strong feelings for him, but I knew we shared similar goals and values, and he also loved my girls." They married and, despite having some rough times between them, they were good co-parents, and the girls were happy. "I was determined to stay because I was looking out for my children's best interest, not my own."

Twenty-five years later, Jeannie says she's "madly in love" with her husband and thinks he is one of the most amazing men on the planet. They have five grandchildren, and Jeannie is happy she gave her girls the gift of a loving stepdad.

Although Jeannie's husband didn't have children of his own when they tied the knot, blended families are increasingly common nowadays. Despite that, many still buy into the stereotypes of the evil stepparent. Sadly, some stepparents are indeed evil, giving rise to the concept of the Cinderella Effect—that people who are biologically unrelated to the children in their care will be less loving to them. Studies appear to confirm that theory; children suffer more abuse from stepparents, typically stepdads, than anyone else.

What Jeannie was able to do for her daughters was to focus on her potential mate's parenting values—not whether he was going to fulfill her sexual and emotional needs. Of course, the majority of stepparents aren't evil; most mean well and try hard. Still, melding a new person into a family, perhaps with kids of his or her own, is often fraught with complications and drama. That is why a Parenting Marriage is an ideal marital model for single parents looking to marry again. You will know that the person you are asking to love your children, care for your children, pay attention to your children, and embrace your children as their own really wants to do that—and, more important, knows *how* to do it.

CHANGING YOUR JOB DESCRIPTION

What if you are already married? In her work, Susan has helped dozens of close-to-divorcing couples transform their relationship from one faltering from arguments, resentments, and a sense of hopelessness to something much more workable for both spouses— a Parenting Marriage.

Take Lanie and Monica, two lesbians in their forties who fell in love and got married in 2005. After they adopted their daughter Mia in 2007, their relationship subsequently went downhill to the point where they could barely tolerate each other's presence. Tensions were high, but neither woman wanted to be the one to leave. They were concerned that Mia, then seven years old, would feel abandoned, and neither wanted that to happen. So they stayed together and suffered.

Then Lanie met Kelly, and it seemed like a natural time to step out of the marriage. But she couldn't go. "There are two reasons I couldn't leave: The first was that I was afraid I'd scar my daughter for life and she'd never forgive me, and the second was, I didn't want to miss out on tucking Mia in each night." Not only that, but the financial reality was something they couldn't escape, after losing their home in the Great Recession.

Monica knew that Lanie had started dating Kelly, but she didn't care. As far as she was concerned, their marriage was dead and had been for a long time—long enough for her to grieve its loss. She was relieved to have Lanie out of the house more and was in a better mood when she was home. Kelly knew about Monica and was fine with the setup, too. Lanie and Monica were able to give their marriage a new purpose instead of breaking up the family unit. They changed their focus from a love relationship to one where they focused on co-mothering Mia.

In the beginning, Lanie felt self-conscious and she didn't want anyone to know—especially Mia. Part of her reluctance to be more open about it was she wasn't sure her new relationship would last, and she was terrified to share the truth. But this made her feel like she was being hypocritical and living a lie. Eventually, she realized that her seven-year-old daughter would view it as acceptable if she did, too. She also began embracing the idea that she didn't need to apologize or justify her choices to anyone outside the family.

When the two moms eventually shared with Mia that they were not an in-love-couple anymore and that Lanie had a new special person who might come over sometimes, Mia's biggest concern was that they wouldn't all stay together. They assured her that she wouldn't have to move and that they'd all still be a family, just with a new member. As they hoped for, Mia was fine with that.

Another middle-aged couple from Northern California that came to the brink of divorce was Greg and Kathy. Both had been married before, but they believed being older and presumably wiser they'd have the marriage thing figured out this time.

Kathy had two kids from her previous marriage; Greg had none, which immediately made him feel like a bit of an outsider. They had a son together fairly soon after their wedding, and Kathy hoped that would help Greg feel more included. It helped, but it wasn't enough: the complications brought on by the two older children having a different dad and having a closer relationship with Kathy than with him continually made him feel pushed out of the inner circle. Life was tolerable until their son turned seven and the resentments that had been building couldn't be contained anymore. One day, they had a huge blowup, and Greg moved out. Divorce seemed inevitable.

After eighteen months of living apart, Greg realized that, although he had felt like an outsider before the split, living apart made him feel much more isolated. His loneliness was far worse after he left, even though he got to see the kids fairly often. Greg realized that Kathy had been the social connection for him when they were married, and, without that, he had virtually no contact with friends. He swallowed his pride and called his estranged wife one day, asking if he could move back in—not as her husband, but more as a roommate and co-parent. Given how hard Kathy found it to make ends meet financially, she welcomed him back.

Both knew it was important to have written agreements in place to delineate things like how to handle parenting responsibilities, finances, and caring for the household. They also talked about how to handle this change with their kids and with friends and extended family. They decided that the inner workings of their relationship wasn't anyone's business, so they agreed that they would keep their unusual arrangement under wraps except with their closest friends. That was five years ago.

Kathy believes it works well. "We stay out of each other's way, we respect one another and don't have heaps of unresolved anger toward each other. We've learned to deal with conflicts as they arise and not let things fester. That helps immensely."

While neither dates, they are free to do so with certain parameters, including not bringing a paramour into their house. Both believe life is so much easier now than when they lived on their own, but, as Kathy says, "I'm sure this arrangement would not have worked if we had not had the year and a half apart." The time gave them the perspective they needed to move back in together in a different way. They don't know what the future holds, especially when their son goes off to college in eight years, but they aren't worried. They know they will figure out the next move as the time gets closer, just as they figured out the other challenges they faced along the way.

YOU CAN MARRY, DIVORCE, AND REMARRY—FOR THE KIDS

Claire and Jorge, a Connecticut couple, divorced not long after their son was diagnosed with autism. Both were in their thirties at the time, and their children were young.

Both worked full time, Claire as a sales rep for an insurance company and Jorge as a law professor at a local college, but guess who had the bulk of the childcare responsibilities? Claire, as is often the case in dual-income couples. "This was challenging enough to our marriage, but having a special-needs child made everything exponentially harder," Claire says. "Not only wasn't [Jorge] helping, he was one more person who needed me to take care of them, and I just couldn't do it." No matter how many times she asked Jorge to help, he always had the same excuse: "I have to work late." Her anger began to fester and grow until she told Jorge he needed to leave. Then she filed for divorce.

Not realizing what he had until Claire threatened him with the "D" word—and not wanting to lose the life he had built with Claire—Jorge begged her to go to counseling with him, promising that he would turn his behavior around. Claire pursued the divorce and reluctantly agreed to go talk to someone, although now she harbored additional resentment over the fact that he had ignored her for so long and it took getting to this point before he was willing to change.

Because of their son's disability, as well as his increased involvement in caring for the kids, Jorge never actually moved out of the family house, even after their dissolution was finalized. Rather than getting worse, things between them actually improved. Jorge stepped up his paternal responsibilities, and Claire saw that they made a really good co-parenting team. Two years passed, and their coordinated efforts of raising their five-year-old daughter and three-year-old autistic son together continued to work well. On what would have been their ninth wedding anniversary, they decided to get remarried.

That was fifteen years ago. Their marriage is actually stronger today than ever before, and both kids are happy, healthy, and well adjusted. Their children have genuinely benefited from their parents coming back together in this new way.

An important lesson that all these couples learned is that how they feel about their partner is much less important than how they act toward the other.

Whether you believe divorce is the worst thing in the world for kids or that divorce can help kids become resilient, one thing is for certain—divorce (and living separately) changes kids' lives in significant ways. Children may lose or have inconsistent or unwanted contact with a parent, they may have to move, they may experience a decrease in financial security, and they may become part of new families with stepparents and half siblings.

Some kids do much better after divorce, while others develop problems that continue throughout their lives.

Divorce isn't bad or good per se; how kids manage post-divorce depends on a lot of variables, not the least of which is whether the parents are fighting. It's the screaming and tension between the parents that does the most harm to children.

Generally speaking, the children who fare better after divorce are the ones who are relieved to be away from the animosity; children who fare worse, in most cases, didn't see their parents fighting, so they didn't know there was anything wrong. These are the children who resist their new reality most and who have the hardest time with their parents' split. Still, divorce seems to have long-lasting effects if it occurs when children are five years old and younger, which speaks even more to our reasoning to have parents commit to staying together until their kids are older.

No matter where you stand on divorce, we believe it's best to create a healthy, stable, child-focused marriage so kids won't have to go through a divorce. That's one of the goals of a Parenting Marriage, as traditional marriage doesn't quite seem up to the task.

MAKING A PARENTING MARRIAGE WORK

You've already seen how couples in existing marriages were able to rethink their roles—or "job descriptions"—for the sake of their children, but without being miserable about it. If you're thinking about getting married because you are unequivocal in your desire to have kids, you will have to readjust your expectations of marriage and your mate. For one, you would need to think more like the gay men mentioned earlier—you'd want to unhitch your sexual and romantic desires from your domestic ones. Rather than find a forever soul mate who fulfilled your every need (and those are tough to find, anyway), you'd look for a mate who would be a good co-parent. Rather than fiery love being the foundation of your union, you'd place a higher priority on finding a good mother or a good father—someone you could trust, respect, and cooperate and collaborate with, who shared goals and interests as it pertained to children and parenting. Fewer demands would be put on each other for affection and attention, but caring for one another and a sense of having each other's back would be no less a priority.

All this may sound boring and highly unromantic when compared with the hype and focus given to marriage nowadays, although entering into a Parenting Marriage doesn't mean you couldn't have the wedding you've always dreamed of. Rather than fret about whether you'll find The One while your or your partner's biological clock ticks away, or settling for someone because you're afraid you won't find someone in time, you might want to ask yourself if it would be satisfying and fulfilling to marry for the main purpose of raising well-adjusted children in a stable and consistent environment.

Millennials (those born between 1980 and 2000, give or take a few years) already believe that being a good parent matters more than having a successful marriage. We think they—and you—can have both, as long as you change your definition of what a successful marriage is. We believe a successful marriage for couples that want to be parents is a Parenting Marriage. Once you have done that, you are free to go separate ways feeling good about how you've just spent the last twenty or so years. Of course, you could also renegotiate your contract into any of the other models in the book and stay together. But if you didn't, you still will have had a successful marriage by your definition of success, ending in a natural dissolution without any of the drama or expense of a divorce. More important, you will have modeled for your children a kind, caring, respectful, and present relationship that gave them what they needed.

We are aware that this model may be upsetting to some people, especially those who cannot or do not want to remove love from the marital equation. They forget that many divorced couples— couples that no longer are in love with each other—are wonderful co-parents when they put their children's needs first. They forget that gays and lesbians, who for so many years were unable to marry and who often had complex family arrangements with surrogate moms and sperm-donor dads, have been wonderful co-parents regardless. In case you haven't noticed, over-the-top weddings, gold wedding bands, and marriage certificates do not bind a couple; having children together does.

WHAT DO YOU TELL THE KIDS?

Some of you may be wondering how to explain what you're doing to the kids. This question assumes that your kids will think something is wrong with what you're doing because you're different than other families. Actually, what usually happens is this: kids take their cues on how to view something from you. If *you* are embarrassed or feel guilt or shame about your parenting arrangement, your children will learn that it is something to keep hidden or be ashamed of (even if you never say anything about it). If, however, you treat your lifestyle in a very matter-of-fact way, your children will hold it as no big deal.

Rachel Hope was actually pleasantly surprised when her son went to a public school and fit in seamlessly with his peers. She had homeschooled him for years, fearing that Jesse might be teased and ostracized. Ironically, the exact opposite happened. Because Rachel and Glenn were comfortable with their choice to be co-parents, Jesse was, too. When he talked about his family to his new high school pals, they were actually jealous!

Adults, however, may not be jealous, or even generous in their assessment of a Parenting Marriage. But divorced people who are successfully co-parenting don't feel any shame; they actually feel pretty good about giving their kids what they need—two parents who love them even if they no longer love each other. You should feel that way, too. Remember, you are agreeing (in exhausting and exacting detail) to give your children a stable, respectful, close, and intact family. If you're as serious as we are about removing any stigma around what are basically private decisions—how and why you choose to marry— then you need to embrace your decision. And guess what—your children will thank you for it.

WHAT'S GOOD ABOUT A PARENTING MARRIAGE

- You will provide a stable environment for children.

- Most of the complicated tasks of parenting will be thought out and planned for before the child is born.

- You will avoid the decrease in marital happiness that occurs for new parents, as your expectations for the marriage will be different.

- You will be free of the pressure to "work" on the marriage.

- A purpose-driven marriage is less precarious than one that's emotion-based.

- By choosing a co-parent carefully, you will be confident in his or her parenting values and styles, and abilities.

- You will feel confident that your partner is as committed to your children as you are.

- Raising children with someone else relieves many of the financial burdens and time constraints of single parenting.

- Having a time limit allows a natural ending to the marriage without the expense and drama of a divorce.

- Since the marriage is not based on love, co-parents may have the freedom to have their sexual and emotional needs fulfilled elsewhere.

- Co-parents can live apart or together as long as both stick to their agreement on time with the children.

- You will be less likely to "spouse bash."

- There will be less conflict about parenting decisions.

- A marriage based on respect and mutual goals, not love, is less volatile.

- Your marital expectations will be grounded, not unrealistic.

- Each spouse will be freer to pursue his or her goals, passions, activities, friendships, and hobbies separately.

- A Parenting Marriage is more egalitarian, with clearly defined tasks.

- There is a greater sense that each spouse is willing to sacrifice for the benefit of the bigger goal, their children.

- Focusing on a potential mate's parenting values and style makes blending families easier and more successful.
- You will model for your kids a partnership based on shared values, affection, kindness, generosity, and friendship.
- If co-parents agree to have their sexual needs filled elsewhere, they will not experience infidelity.
- Your children will be much less likely to worry about you and your spouse.
- Your children will likely grow up without a lot of parental conflict.
- Your children will likely experience a home without criticism, sarcasm, defensiveness, or passive-aggressive behavior.

WHAT'S NOT SO GOOD ABOUT A PARENTING MARRIAGE

- You will likely face judgment and misunderstanding from society at large as well as family, friends, and coworkers.
- Your kids might be teased because their family arrangement is outside the norm.
- The true impact on children of a partnership not based on love is not fully known.
- Having outside lovers may complicate the relationship dynamics.
- Taking romantic love out of the equation doesn't prevent the possibility that you still may grow apart.
- You may feel like your relationship is less "we" and "us" focused because that strong romantic love bond isn't there.
- You may have mixed emotions about missing out on a passionate marriage.
- You may feel jealous of what you perceive as other people's "happy" marriages.
- You may feel your marriage is "less than" others.
- You may feel that you settled.
- You may still be disappointed, frustrated, or unhappy about your co-parenting partner.

- You may not be able to fight the feeling that it is not the fairytale marriage you might have hoped for.

- You may have a hard time finding others to fulfill your sexual and emotional needs.

- You may miss the feeling of being loved and loving someone back.

- You may feel that you've sacrificed too much for your children.

- You or your partner might change your mind about the situation.

HOW TO MAKE A PARENTING MARRIAGE WORK

Of all the marriages we've outlined in this book, this is the marriage that requires the most conscious commitment to having a good co-parenting relationship. Your job description in this marriage is to be the best parent you can be to your child or children.

This marriage may be right for you if:

- You both have a strong desire to have and raise a child.

- You both understand what it means to raise a child.

- You place your children's mental, physical, and emotional welfare first wherever possible.

- You know and trust your co-parent.

- You have common goals and agreeable parenting styles.

- You have a mutually agreed upon Co-Parenting Agreement outlining who takes care of what, and a plan of action that includes such things as custody and financial responsibilities, discipline, dietary and health issues, schooling, religion, extracurricular activities, etc.

- You agree to revisit and adjust the Co-Parenting Agreement regularly and to communicate frequently as issues arise.

- You and your co-parent each have a will, a living trust, or both.

- You are flexible, compassionate, open-minded, patient, dedicated, and respectful.

- You are able to communicate clearly and non-defensively.

- You're a good listener.

- You have good problem-solving skills.

- You are good at resolving conflict with compassion and respect.

- You can be supportive of your partner even if you don't agree.

- You know how to be part of a team and value that over individual needs.

- You do everything you can to have a healthy environment in the home.

- If you do not plan to live with your co-parent, you each agree to keep the rules and expectations the same in both homes.

- You are mature and can handle your own delayed gratification.

- You will make sure there is a realistic and adequate spending plan in place for each of your children's future.

- You agree to seek help from experts in the event that you run into parenting or co-parenting challenges.

- You will maintain your own health and wellness regime.

- You will do everything you can to model healthy adult behaviors in your relationship.

IS A PARENTING MARRIAGE RIGHT FOR ME?

Wondering if you're cut out for a Parenting Marriage? Here are a few questions you might want to ask yourself (some may not be applicable if you are already married and are seeking to renegotiate your marriage):

- How important is it for me to have children?

- Why do I want to have a child?

- What are my most treasured childhood memories?

- What are my worst childhood memories?

- In what way would I want to parent like my parents did?

- In what way would I not want to parent like my parents did?

- What about co-parenting with a mate excites me?
- What scares me?
- What would I gain from this kind of marriage?
- What would I miss?
- What qualities should a good parent have?
- Why would I make a good parent?
- What other qualities would I want in a co-parenting spouse besides shared values and beliefs about children?
- How important is it for me to be in love with my spouse?
- How important to me is it to be loved back?
- Do I believe love can last a lifetime?
- Do I believe a marriage must have love?
- How important is independence and freedom to me?
- What are my top five non-negotiable parenting values?
- Why would a Parenting Marriage be a better option for me than a traditional lifelong commitment?
- Why would a Parenting Marriage be a better option for me than being a single parent by choice?
- Would I prefer to live with my co-parenting spouse or not?
- How hands-on do I want my co-parenting spouse to be?
- How important is it to have my co-parenting spouse be monogamous?
- Do I want to get my sexual and emotional needs met elsewhere?
- Would I be able to get my sexual and emotional needs met elsewhere?
- Would I really be able to put my needs behind those of my children?
- How easy or hard would it be for me to commit to eighteen years or more with a person I may not love?
- What do I think about divorce?
- How would I feel knowing that the marriage has a term limit?

READ MORE

Curious about how to make this marital model work? Here are some books to read for insight and guidance:

- *Family by Choice: Platonic Partnered Parenting* by Rachel Hope (Word Birth Publishing, 2014).
- *Family by Design: The Complete Guide to Successfully Finding a Parenting Partner and Navigating the Co-Parenting Process* by Darren R. Spedale (Self, 2014).
- *Gay Marriage: For Better or for Worse?: What We've Learned from the Evidence* by William N. Eskridge Jr. and Darren R. Spedale (Oxford University Press, 2006).
- *Parent-Child Relations: An Introduction to Parenting* (ninth edition) by Jerry J. Bigner and Clara J. Gerhardt (Pearson, 2013).
- *Partnership Parenting: How Men and Women Parent Differently—Why It Helps Your Kids and Can Strengthen Your Marriage* by Kyle Pruett, MD, and Marsha Pruett, PhD, (Da Capo Lifelong Books, 2009).
- *The Single Girl's Guide to Marrying a Man, His Kids, and His Ex-Wife: Becoming a Stepmother with Humor and Grace* by Sally Bjornsen (NAL Trade, 2005).

PARENTING MARRIAGE TAKEAWAYS

- A Parenting Marriage is "kid-centric," meaning the main purpose of this marriage is to raise a child or children.

- It's the epitome of "planned parenthood."

- Those who enter into a Parenting Marriage commit to stay together until the kids are independent.

- A Parenting Marriage requires you to unhitch your romantic and sexual desires from your domestic responsibilities.

- The threat of divorce is greatly minimized.

- Couples are better prepared for the tremendous task of being a parent.

- It is an ideal way to satisfy the biological clock if you haven't met The One.

- Kids need a peaceful, respectful environment in order to thrive, not parents who love each other.

Chapter 6

LIVING ALONE TOGETHER:

DISTANCE MAKES THE HEART GROW FONDER

⏺————————————————————————————⏺

"Don't tell me long-distance relationships don't work out because
as far as I can see, local relationships don't work any better."
—Anonymous

ariel expected things would change when she got married. Except they really didn't. Instead of living together as a blissful happy newlywed couple, Mariel and her husband, Tim, continued the same pattern they had throughout their engagement—they lived hundreds of miles apart, not by choice but because they both couldn't find a decent job in the same county, let alone town.

And that's how it was for about three years, with him traveling to see her every weekend. They talked on the phone every night, there were flirty—and dirty—texts, and there was phone sex. And then, on the weekends, there was real sex. Okay—newlyweds certainly should be bonking each other at every opportunity. But for the couple, the weekends were beyond exciting. "When I hadn't seen him for a week, that first kiss just swept me off my feet," she says with a glowing smile.

While Mariel was extremely happy when Tim found a job close to hers and they could finally live together in the San Francisco Bay Area, she learned a lot during the years when they lived apart: "I definitely know that I'm going to need days that I can go out with the girls or do something on my own because I need some space to do my own thing, and he does, too."

They had a Living Alone Together, or LAT, marriage, also called Living Apart Together or a Commuter Marriage. We wouldn't encourage you to choose a LAT marriage because you've "had enough," as you saw Vicki's mother did in the introduction. But we're all for you choosing a LAT marriage—or giving each other space in your existing marriage—because it offers you and your partner exactly what you want: connection and intimacy with enough freedom to avoid the claustrophobia that often comes with living together 24/7 as well as whatever it is that makes many people take each other for granted, whether they're married or cohabiting.

THE BEST OF BOTH WORLDS

Familiarity breeds contempt, or so the saying goes (backed by studies), and contempt is one of the famed "Four Horsemen of the Apocalypse" that relationship expert and psychologist John Gottman has determined will kill a marriage.

Not every marriage has contempt, thankfully. But many spouses do not encourage and support individual growth and freedom, for themselves or their partners. Most people don't equate marriage with "freedom." That's what people have when they're single, right? If anything, marriage curtails freedom and holds people accountable to their partner and society, which we explored in Chapter 2. Wives especially feel the freedom crunch. More wives than husbands say they don't have enough space to themselves, in part because women tend to do more of the caregiving, even if they work outside the home, too (in fact, they spend twice as much time as men doing "family care"). For whatever reason, men still tend to have more leisure time than women (or are better at making that happen). Even so, both rank the lack of privacy or time to focus on themselves as a reason that they're unhappy in their marriage—almost twice as many as those who say they are unhappy because of their sex life.

Living separately from your partner can give you the best of both worlds. In fact, there may be a lot more to gain from it than to lose. Anyone who grew up in a large family or in a household where there was a great deal of discord understandably might choose a LAT marriage. "Young people are seeing that the old way of doing things isn't working, and they're experimenting with how to fix it," writes *The Business of Love* author John Curtis.

Not everyone is cut out to live with other people. It doesn't mean they don't want commitment or a relationship. Couples that don't want to live together are often seen as fearing intimacy, laments Judye Hess, sixty-nine, a Berkeley, California, family therapist who lives around the block from her long-time boyfriend in an arrangement she likes to call dual dwelling duos. She rejects societal pressure to be coupled in a narrowly defined way—two people, one place—and believes fewer couples would struggle in their romantic relationships if they saw living apart as a viable option.

We agree with her.

For some people, their career is their life. While they love their family, their biggest satisfaction comes from the work they do and the recognition they get from it—as well as the nice paycheck. Perhaps you're one of them. Being able to devote yourself fully to your career without having to deal with the many needs and dramas of a spouse and family life on a daily basis feels pretty good. So does having extended chunks of freedom and a room of one's own, so to speak. Sometimes, spouses live on opposite sides of the country, meaning visits home don't happen that often and don't last that long.

The husband of one couple we know flew weekly to New York City, where he was the CEO of a big pharmaceutical distribution firm. He traveled from the sprawling family home outside San Francisco every Sunday night and returned home every Friday night. His wife was left to attend to their two young sons as well as pretty much everything else kid- and home-related, turning her into what many consider a "super-parent." Admittedly, it was hard on her and the kids despite the help of a housekeeper and gardener. And it was hard on him. But as a family with strong traditional values, they decided it was the best arrangement for them, and they continued living like that for many years.

Not all LATs are driven by careers, although, thanks to the economic downturn, more couples have had to reluctantly live apart for their jobs, as in Mariel and Tim's case. While an unintended long-distance marriage may add great stress to couples that would prefer to live under the same roof, there are a few unexpected perks, as Mariel shared earlier. Still, it's much more preferable if a couple willingly chooses to live apart because it fits who they are and how they like to spend their time, alone and together. And it's those perks that make us believe that a LAT marriage offers a lot of answers to the never-ending struggle married couples face—how to create a sense of freedom and independence and not lose your sense of personal identity while also having a loving, intimate partnership and perhaps a better sexual relationship. Studies indicate that women who don't live with their partners retain their desire much more than women who do.

LAT IS NOT ANOTHER WORD FOR SELFISH

So, who are LATs, and what do they look like? Some LATs live apart only a few days during the week; others live apart half the year. Some live apart by choice; some—like those who get deployed overseas—because duty or a special assignment calls.

They could look like Mariel and Tim, who never wanted to live apart but were forced to temporarily because they couldn't find work close by. They can look like Jane and John, who are in their second marriage and are established in their careers on different coasts and choose to remain working. They can look like Vicki's parents, then-empty-nesters who lived apart by choice in different states for a long time for personal fulfillment (well, at least her mother's). They can also look like couples that live next door or down the block from each other or in separate parts of their house and then arrange how often they spend time together.

In other words, they don't all look the same—each arrangement is flexible and mutually agreed upon to suit each partner's needs. Which, of course, brings up some obvious questions: Shouldn't spouses put aside their own needs (and freedom) for the betterment of the couple? Isn't that one of the basic reasons for getting married—because two people want to spend their lives together and bring out the best in each other while celebrating togetherness? Where is the "togetherness" when you're living apart?

Those are valid questions. However, "togetherness" doesn't always lead to more intimacy and warm and fuzzy feelings about your spouse.

Here's what Jane, sixty-three, and John, sixty-nine, have to say about tying the knot after they'd been together for four years. John, who was widowed after forty-three years of marriage, lives and works on the East Coast. Jane, who divorced after twenty-eight years of marriage, lives and works on the West Coast. Their first marriages were traditional, but their new arrangement is anything but. The couple met through work, and each time Jane flew to the East Coast to meet with John, a consultant, she was impressed with his easy-going personality and his smarts. After many months, they realized they had a spark together.

They spend about 30 percent of their time together, mostly flying to the opposite coast or sometimes meeting somewhere in between, and they never spend more than two weekends apart. They believe this arrangement gives them the best of both worlds (and the best part, they both agree, is when they get to see each other again).

Both are passionate about their careers and wouldn't have much to offer each other at the end of their exhausting days if they lived together anyway—except perhaps some "meaningful" conversations about who's taking out the garbage, Jane says with a laugh. Living apart relieves them from the daily friction that they both believe would be inevitable because of their different ways of doing things.

"During our weekends, we do everything together," Jane says. "With my other marriage, we were in the house together all week long, but we had a tenth of the level of intimacy. . . . I think, frankly, there's something wrong with traditional marriage, that day in and day out you see the same person, and the little things that can annoy become sort of standard annoyances. . . . It's nice to have a very full life so that when we are apart, there's not one of us feeling, oh, I'm left out and I'm lonely and I'm unhappy and he or she is not there for me, because then you feel the discontent."

As Jane beautifully points out, just because you're living together doesn't mean that you are always engaging with each other in significant ways. In fact, about half of the two or so hours couples spend together every day are spent watching TV. There is nothing intimacy-building or meaningful about that (unless watching a show about someone else's hard times or dysfunctional marriage helps you appreciate how easy your life together is). Even if you're not engaging, though, at least you are in the same physical space. You eat dinner together. You share details of the day, no matter how trivial. We get it; it's hard not to think that is how a marriage "should" look. How else can you stay committed, grow more intimate, and trust each other when you don't see each other all the time? You may be surprised to learn that researchers who've looked at how couples maintain LAT relationships have found that couples feel as stable, satisfied, committed, and trusting as couples that live together do. Often, they have even higher levels of stability, satisfaction, commitment, and trust.

IS THE DOOR OPEN TO TROUBLE?

How do you make sure you have a strong LAT marriage? Let's start with trust first because most people would say it's the biggie. Trust, we're sure you will agree, is key in a relationship. When your partner is around you 24/7, you kind of know what he's doing (for the sake of simplicity, we'll stick to masculine pronouns, but we're talking about either gender). You know his coworkers and friends; you know whom he has lunch with during the week and whom he goes mountain biking with on the weekends. You know the attractive and shapely new coworker who tends to wear clingy dresses and who was a little too friendly at last year's holiday party. You know his former college roomie, a perpetual bachelor and quintessential pickup artist who frequently calls your hubby for a night out to re-create their old partying ways. And you know the woman he carpools to work with every day, a recent divorcée in her forties with a ten-year-old daughter who entertains him with her funny stories of post-divorce dating and sex. You know them because he talks about them and you've most likely met them. In other words, you know the cast of characters in his life.

This is not always so if you live miles or states apart. While you may have heard the names and stories of the new coworker, the carpool driver, and the old college buddy who lives near your husband's office, you have no idea who they really are, what they look like, and how they act. You may not have visuals, and, because many people size up another person's trustworthiness by his or her face, you can't quite assess whether that person is in some way a "threat" to your marriage. Obviously, not everyone struggles with this sort of thing. Some couples are secure in their relationship and can easily and playfully banter about whom they find attractive, whom they would want to sleep with if they could, and the kind of flirting they engage in. But other couples cannot readily contain their jealousy. We explore the complicated—and necessary—emotion more in depth in the chapter on Open Marriage, but jealousy can grow when you live apart from your partner because there is too much you don't know and too much you perceive as out of your control.

Of course, the same jealousy can occur when your partner lives with you. If you have ever "accidently" scrolled through your partner's emails or cell phone text messages, if you have ever asked (in as innocent a voice as you can muster), "Who were you just talking to on the phone?" or if you have ever uttered in the car on the way home from a party (after having spent the entire time seething), "Do you think I'm blind? What in the world were you doing talking to that blonde for so long?" well, you know what we mean.

Distance can make the heart grow fonder, but distance can also make your mind wander: Would he cheat on me? It's just too easy to fool around when each of you is doing your own thing. And that means you, too. If you're living apart from your spouse, it's understandable that you may feel lonely sometimes. Maybe you're not thinking about cheating, but one day you meet someone you're attracted to, or your first love, whom you've kept in contact with on Facebook, is in town on business and wants to meet for a drink. The next thing you know, the two of you are going at it in your marital bed or at a nearby hotel suite.

It happens. Except you also know that it happens when spouses live together, too. The number of couples that are "married, spouse absent," according to the United States census, is a lot less than the numbers of couples living together—just a little over 3 percent of the population. It's hard to get an exact number of how many people have affairs because it is all self-reported. But it doesn't really make a difference what percent it is; it's obvious that living together doesn't prevent anyone from having an affair. So, does living apart make it "easier"? It sure seems like it could; after all, there are separate living spaces that are just "mine" and "yours," there is a lot more time spent alone, and it would be a lot less complicated to hide any extramarital shenanigans. Not to mention, loneliness could rear its ugly head at any time.

"People who commute a lot or travel a lot for business can almost have separate lives," Tina B. Tessina, author of *The Commuter Marriage*, tells us. "There's a lot of chatter about 'work spouses,' that work partner who seems close enough to be a spouse because you work on so many projects together. In actuality, that often becomes a reality, especially if the 'work spouses' travel together."

That still doesn't mean someone is going to be unfaithful, and some recent studies indicate that missing your partner may actually make you feel even *more* faithful. And, like an Open Marriage, LAT marriages help people cope with the uncertainties that come with romantic relationships. You are basically forced to contend with your insecurities, and for many, that leads to greater introspection and self-awareness.

While those choosing a long-distance marriage may not end up having to deal with an affair any more or less than those who live together, they do tend to think about it more. And because of that, addressing monogamy and infidelity may be a more frequent conversation between those couples, which cannot hurt and actually can help. Ultimately, what it comes down to is this: are you marrying or are you married to someone you trust, and is that person worthy of your trust? And, are you offering the same? Because if you can't trust your partner, whatever living arrangement you have isn't going to change the situation. It isn't *how* you live (together or apart); it's *whom* you live with.

"I WANT MY INTIMACY!"

This brings us to intimacy, which most people would say is the other important piece of the puzzle. How can you maintain, let alone build, intimacy when you're not around each other all the time? In days past, people wrote long, elaborate love letters to each other, letters that often took weeks if not months to reach the beloved. Today, there's technology, like it or not (and perhaps the occasional "I love you" note tucked in a suitcase).

Maybe you can't stand texting. Maybe you refuse to participate in the often seemingly self-absorbed displays on Facebook. Maybe things like Instagram and Snapchat just make you nervous. And maybe you grow weary trying to stay up with how quickly technology outlets can change. But for all the downsides of how much people use—and often abuse—technology, it has made long-distance living and loving a reality. The once geographically undesirable potential mate (whom you may not have ever met were it not for online dating sites) is someone's wife or husband today. Technology is at the heart of LAT relationships.

Jane and John talk on the phone every day. They text several times a day. On Saturday mornings, they use FaceTime to connect. If anything major happens, they are on the phone or texting, or both, more than usual. They found ways to create intimacy that demand more of them, and it's working. While they laugh about phone sex, admitting they're a bit too old to be focused on that, others may feel differently. Recent innovations and virtual reality technologies such as Fundawear, an app-controlled intercourse simulator, are likely to take long-distance sex to an exciting new level.

It doesn't matter how physically close you are to your partner as long as you both feel as close as you want to be—even if that isn't all that close by other people's standards. As many people who are in LAT relationships, or were in them for a while, say, they learned some valuable relationship skills, including trust, patience, and better communication. Many also got better at time management, independence, and discovering intimacy that wasn't just about sex and touch.

All of those skills can lead to a more satisfying relationship, and relationship satisfaction can make couples feel more committed to each other. Couples that feel committed to each other are motivated to show it; they act in ways that their partner can clearly experience as loving. And they don't need to be under the same roof to act loving.

Isn't that exactly what people want in a marriage? Once the wild sex and lust of an early relationship dies down—usually around two years—then emotional commitment often ties a couple together, but not always happily. Haven't you seen couples that stay together in loveless, sexless marriages because they muttered, "until death do us part," some ten, fifteen, twenty years ago? Their relationship isn't satisfying anymore, they no longer act loving to each other—or they rarely do—but they slog along anyway. That isn't the kind of commitment we encourage.

Remembering how it felt when they lived apart helps remind Mariel how lucky she is to have her husband. "I've thought about it, how I need to remember this, that he's really special to me and I need to think about that every day."

We agree. That said, a LAT Marriage might not be for everyone. It certainly isn't a good fit if you need to have someone around you all you the time and if you struggle with trust and intimacy issues. It may work well for people who have a strong sense of self and independence, people who are able to feel committed and intimate despite periods of time apart, and people who are resilient in times of stress and challenges.

MAKING A ROOM OF YOUR OWN

If you're in a marriage and want to create more space, you can do what Vicki's mom did—announce that you need your freedom (and that it's not open for discussion), gather up your stuff, and set up a new life elsewhere. But we don't recommend you do it quite that way. Still, taking time away from your marriage may be a way to step back and give each other time to breathe, without destroying your family's stability if you're at an impasse in your relationship.

Assuming you are not considering becoming a LAT for career purposes, you need to question your motivations. Do you see this as a first step to a divorce, or as a way to experience yourself in a new light and as your own person, somewhat loosened from the yoke of "wife" or "husband"? Do you see it as a way to create a healthy distance from your spouse so you can rediscover what you fell in love with in the first place and so you can reunite with the intention of enjoying each other's company in new ways?

Once you're clear on your motivations, you need to envision what it's going to look like. Do you want to move into the family home's in-law unit? Rent an apartment down the block? Move to another city, maybe closer to your aging parents or a beloved relative? House-sit a friend's condo on Maui for a few months while she's on an overseas assignment?

Then you have to be realistic about your situation. Do you have children still at home? Are you financially able to handle it? And, just as important, are you and your spouse emotionally able to handle it?

Finally, you need a plan of action. How long will you be away? How often will you see each other—if at all—and who will come to whom? By what means will you keep in touch, and how frequently?

Then comes the hard part—sharing your thoughts with your spouse, lovingly, respectfully, and honestly. It may go over well; it may not. Maybe he has long been secretly entertaining a similar idea; maybe she'll get angry and accuse you of having an affair. It may take some time for emotions to work themselves out before it can be discussed again. And you have to be prepared for the fact that it not only may lead to a flat-out rejection—and then what will you do?—but it also may cause a fracture in your marriage. A neutral third party might need to be called on to help.

Ideally, the decision should be a mutual one, and talking about the benefits both of you may experience will go a lot further than basing the arrangement on fulfilling just your needs.

WHAT IF YOU'RE ALREADY MARRIED— WITH KIDS?

Now, about the kids. Obviously, if you don't have children and you want to transition to a LAT marriage, there's a lot less to think about and negotiate. Kids complicate everything. We aren't going to talk you out of living apart if you have kids at home—certainly enough couples are forced to live that way for work or because a spouse is in the armed services. There are structures that can be set up to have your children's lives continue on as normal, or as close to what they've come to know as normal. However, everyone is bound to react emotionally when you tell your child that "Mommy and Daddy aren't going to live together like we have been."

In many ways, it may get the same reaction kids give when their parents pull them aside and tell them they are planning to divorce. Yet, those unhappy conversations happen all the time and children manage (and have even been known to thrive). Finding the right language to explain it to them and reassuring them of your love for them and your spouse is essential. You may want to read up on how divorced parents do it, ask your divorced friends, or talk to a professional.

If you're the commuter, you and your spouse will have to come up with a plan that addresses how you, the absent parent, will maintain meaningful connection with your kids and have everyone feel like you are part of the family. You will also want to be sensitive to your spouse's needs; you really want to avoid the "super-parent" syndrome as much as you can.

Then you will just need to keep communicating. You'll want to be sure to let your kids know when you'll be home again, and assure them that they will have plenty of one-on-one time with you before you leave. In addition to time alone with your child, you'll want to have a lot of family time, too, and deal with whatever work you may have brought home with you after your kids' bedtime. Just think how disheartening it would be for your child to see you on your laptop or taking calls or checking texts and emails throughout the day.

Setting up specific days and times when you can talk on the phone, FaceTime, or Skype with them is essential, too, given kids' jam-packed school schedules and extracurricular activities nowadays. In between, you can text and email. And nothing can replace a handwritten letter or card, which regardless of your child's age becomes a precious gift that can be held, tacked on a wall, and treasured forever.

If you are the parent who is in the home with the kids, make sure your needs are being addressed so you don't start to feel resentful. There haven't been many studies on the long-term effects of LAT marriages on children, but we are pretty sure children may have different experiences if a parent lives apart because of her career versus having separate households for personal freedom within the marriage. A child may be angry or unhappy with both, but less upset if the reason seems "legitimate," or beyond your control. If the reason for living apart is a "choice," a child may take it as rejection and might be angry with one or both parents for being selfish. Others (coworkers, friends, and family) may disapprove of your decision and question your commitment to your family. You may find yourself wondering that, too, as well as feeling pangs of guilt. And you may find that your absence is blamed for anything and everything that goes wrong in your children's lives—from a C-on a math test to the neatly rolled joints found stashed in your teenager's sock drawer.

Again, while these may be challenging, they are not much different than what divorced co-parents and their children experience. These various live-apart scenarios have "proved an effective means of bettering the lot of loved ones although not without substantial costs," write professors Richard Glotzer and Anne Cairns Federlein in a report on commuter marriages, including their own. Just about every decision couples make in creating a life together comes with costs—you will have to decide which costs are worth it.

WHAT'S GOOD ABOUT A LAT MARRIAGE

- LATs have the same or even higher levels of stability than couples that live together.
- LAT couples are as satisfied or are more satisfied with their relationship than couples that live together.
- LAT couples have the same or even higher levels of commitment than couples that live together.
- LATs feel the same amount of trust or more trust for their partner than couples that live together.
- A LAT marriage offers a healthy balance between personal fulfillment and intimacy.
- Living apart often means couples don't focus on the negative and trivial behaviors—uncapped toothpaste tubes or piles of papers, etc.—that sometimes frustrate spouses.
- Couples that live apart don't have the same constraints that living together entails, so it's easy for them to feel more confident that they are in the relationship for the "right" reasons.
- LATs don't feel claustrophobic.
- There may be less conflict.
- Each spouse is freer to pursue his or her own goals, passions, activities, friendships, and hobbies without having to check in with the other partner.
- Each spouse can focus on his or her career.
- Spouses are less likely to feel like they've given up something for their partner.
- Spouses are less likely to feel that they don't have a separate identity from their partner.
- Time spent together is often much more romantic and passionate.
- Sex can be more exciting.
- Marriages tend to be more egalitarian.
- There's a sense that each spouse is willing to sacrifice for the other's benefit.

- If one or both have children from previous relationships, they don't have the stress and complications of blending families.
- It gives couples space to closely re-examine their relationship and find other ways to understand their partner.
- In certain situations, it may give couples time to think things through before responding.
- It helps people better cope with whatever insecurities come with romantic relationships.
- If the marriage dissolves, they still have a place to live and they may handle it better.

WHAT'S NOT SO GOOD ABOUT A LAT MARRIAGE

- You may face judgment and misunderstanding from family, friends, and coworkers.
- It may create emotional distress or uncertainty.
- It can be expensive.
- It can be complicated if you're raising children; the one at home may feel like he/she is doing all the work, and the one away from home may feel disconnected.
- It may be lonely at times.
- You may differ on how much time you should spend apart.
- You may differ on how you'll spend time together.
- It may not feel comfortable to rely on the phone, Skype, email, or other technology to catch up with each other daily.
- You might feel jealous and/or suspicious.
- You may feel a lack of control.
- You can't always have sex when you want it.
- It may be challenging to make joint decisions from afar.
- If you're living apart because of circumstance and not choice, you may feel frustrated and resentful.

- You may start to grow apart.
- You may feel like your relationship is less "we" and "us" focused.
- If you only have limited time together, you may avoid bringing up certain issues that need to be addressed.
- You may feel anxiety.
- You may feel guilt.
- It may be harder to solve disagreements.

HOW TO MAKE A LAT MARRIAGE WORK

- Trust is key.
- You should feel comfortable using technology—texts, email, Skype, Face-Time, etc.—as well as phone calls and "snail mail" (how romantic is it to get a card or letter in the mailbox!) to feel connected.
- You see intimacy as more than physical contact and presence.
- You are in a good financial standing and are able to take on two households.
- You are mature and emotionally stable.
- You have a stable, egalitarian relationship.
- You need to be actively engaged in work or other pursuits that occupy your time and mental energy.
- You need to be flexible.
- You need to be a good communicator.
- You need to be reliable.
- You should be comfortable with ambiguity.
- You are efficient at planning and time use.
- You enjoy time alone.
- You like being independent, and you like your partner to be independent.
- You are okay with gently ignoring or responding to how others perceive your marriage.

IS A LAT MARRIAGE RIGHT FOR ME?

Wondering if you're cut out for a LAT Marriage? Here are a few questions you might want to ask yourself (some may not be applicable if you are already married and are seeking to renegotiate your marriage):

- What about living apart excites me?

- What scares me?

- What would I gain?

- What would I miss?

- Are there other marital arrangements that would give me the same benefits without living apart?

- How flexible am I?

- Can we afford it?

- How long would we want to live apart?

- Would I be able to fully trust my partner?

- How would we keep the intimacy alive?

- Would I want to live apart if we decide to have kids?

- How frequently do we need to see each other for me to feel comfortable?

- Should we have any limits on friendships, especially opposite-sex friendships, when we're apart?

- Do I feel comfortable with my partner's independence?

- Do I feel comfortable being so independent?

- Am I okay not being around my partner all the time?

- Am I okay with whatever hassles I might have to deal with living by myself for periods of time?

- Do we agree on how we'd handle bills, finances, household chores and maintenance, travel costs, who travels to see whom, etc.?

- What would happen if one of us decides it's not working?

READ MORE

Curious about how to make this marital model work? Here are some books to read for insight and guidance:

- *The Commuter Marriage* by Tina B. Tessina (Adams Media, 2008).
- *The Long-Distance Relationship Guide* by Caroline Tiger (Quirk Books, 2007).
- *The Long-Distance Relationship Guidebook* by Sylvia Shipp (Sylvia Shipp, 2007).
- *The Long-Distance Relationship Survival Guide* by Chris Bell and Kate Brauer-Bell (Ten Speed Press, 2006).
- *Long Distance Relationships: The Complete Guide* by Gregory Guldner (JF Milne Publications, 2003).
- *Super Commuter Couples: Staying Together When a Job Keeps You Apart* by Megan Bearce (Eqanimity Press, 2013).
- *A Year by the Sea: Thoughts of an Unfinished Woman* by Joan Anderson (Broadway Books, 2000).

LAT MARRIAGE TAKEAWAYS

- A LAT Marriage is an arrangement where couples keep separate residences all or part of the time.
- In a LAT Marriage, couples can enjoy autonomy as well as couplehood.
- A LAT Marriage is a good option for those starting out in a marriage or those who have been married for a while and "need a break."
- A LAT Marriage encourages growth and freedom within the marriage.
- A LAT Marriage requires strong trust between partners.
- Couples in a LAT Marriage think more consciously about their commitment.
- Together time is often more meaningful in a LAT Marriage.
- Couples in a LAT Marriage often find creative ways to have intimacy.
- Couples in a LAT Marriage learn trust, patience, and better communication skills.

Chapter 7

COVENANT MARRIAGE:

EXTREME MARRIAGE MAKEOVERS

"Success in marriage does not come merely through finding the
right mate, but through being the right mate."
—Barnett Brickner

There you are, finally standing before your friends and loved
ones with your sweetheart, vowing to be together for better
and worse, for richer and poorer, in sickness and in health. Before
you got to that altar you spent months, maybe years, planning every
detail—the flowers, your dress, your bridesmaids' dresses, the venue,
the DJ, the videographer . . . well, you get the idea. But one thing that
you didn't plan for was divorce. Nevertheless, a few years after that
lovely wedding, you find yourself divorced. Despite the vows you and
your spouse took that glorious day, it's over. Some people are simply
unwilling or unable to keep those promises.

What happened? What we found in our research is that there
are three types of marriers: those who take their vows seriously and
won't divorce under any circumstances; those who don't take marriage all that seriously and marry and divorce at the drop of a hat
(and nowhere is this more apparent than Hollywood); and, by far the

majority, those who marry with the best intentions to stick to those vows, but who would consider divorce if something egregious happened, like infidelity, abuse, or addiction.

Even as people say their vows, the idea of divorce might be in the back of their minds. As one young bride-to-be told us, she was reluctant to get engaged to her live-in boyfriend of six years "until I realized that if it didn't work out, I could just get divorced. So I said yes." Knowing she had an out enabled her to step in.

But what if it weren't that easy? If you are the type of marrier who doesn't want to leave the back door open to exit when things get a bit more challenging and you want your future spouse to feel the same way, there's a marriage for you. Actually, it isn't just a marriage—it's a separate, legally recognized marriage license. It's a Covenant Marriage.

Maybe you haven't heard of it. Most people we spoke with hadn't heard of it either, unless they were from the South, and even there many had no idea what it was. The South is where Covenant Marriages were born, live, and breathe in the United States: they began in Louisiana in 1997.

The idea of Covenant Marriage dates back to 1947 France. French legislators wanted to combat the increasing number of divorces in the country. In 1947, the divorce rate in the country jumped from an average of 15,000 per year to nearly 58,000 because of changes in laws and postwar upheaval.

It was also seen as a way to assure each member of the couple-to-be that he and she shared the same intention. A debate ensued with the legislators about the realities of life and the inability of anyone to predict what might cause them to divorce, but they could not all agree on how to solve the problem. Some seemed to like the premise and agreed there was a problem that needed to be solved, but they just couldn't get behind the proposal as it was written. The measure lost with a vote of nine to twelve.

In the mid-'90s, the religious and political right in the United States resurrected the indissoluble marriage idea as a way to preserve the sanctity of marriage as well as to bring the divorce rates down.

Conservatives saw the no-fault divorce laws as the number one factor in the mass marital exodus that occurred in the 1970s. Rather than stand by, helpless to do anything about it, they decided to create a marriage that made people really think about what they were getting themselves into.

Certainly, the impact of divorce on society as a whole was important, but it was the children of divorce that mattered more to people like Katherine Spaht, a retired family law professor at Louisiana State University, who helped write one of the original bills. She saw these kids as the innocent victims of their parents' choices, and she wanted couples to take their commitment more seriously. Spaht worked tirelessly to get the fledgling Covenant Marriage law passed through Congress.

Religion plays a large role in the Covenant Marriage movement, which is why many of the less-religiously inclined haven't heard about this option. As a committed Christian, Spaht not only worked on the gubernatorial level to create a stronger marriage but she also worked with local pastors and religious communities to get their backing. There was a great deal of resistance early on, she recalls.

When Louisiana approved Covenant Marriage, "it was the first time in 200 years that marriage laws moved in the opposite direction," she told us proudly. It was also the first time in the history of the postindustrial Western world that people had a choice of marriage models. Only two states followed Louisiana's lead, Arizona in 1998 and Arkansas in 2001, although Covenant Marriage legislation has been proposed and rejected in twenty-five states. And despite Spaht's pride, only about 2 percent have actually chosen to marry that way.

Jennifer and Joe from Arkansas entered into a Covenant Marriage more than a decade ago. Most people hadn't heard of the new marriage then, and, as they acknowledge here, not much has changed since then in that regard: "When we bought our marriage license in 2003, we had to ask for the Covenant Marriage information. We were told that we were the first couple in our county to even ask about it."

Some family members and friends were skeptical about their

Covenant Marriage. "Many thought it was 'wasted' effort because 'who marries with the thought of divorce?' On the plus side, many others were very supportive but had never heard of it. Even after almost ten years, I still have to explain what it is to some, which I do gladly if I'm given the opportunity. In Arkansas, a couple can even convert their marriage to a Covenant Marriage, but again I don't think it is well publicized."

It's not. That's why we included it in our book. We wanted you to know that, in addition to making marriage more pliable, you can also agree to add more legal restrictions to make your marriage stronger and more durable.

Covenant Marriage differs from traditional marriage in two important ways: it's harder to get into and harder to get out of. Instead of just saying, "I do," think of it as saying, "I do. I really, really, really, really do!" Couples that want a Covenant Marriage must participate in premarital counseling with a specially trained clergyperson or therapist to help them understand the level of commitment they are entering into, learn how to manage the challenges of living life on life's terms, and discuss expectations each has of the marriage.

Then they can go to their local courthouse to pick up the necessary basic nuptial documents and a few more—a signed affidavit stating they have completed premarital counseling, an attestation from the person who provided counseling confirming that they completed the program, and a declaration of intent (see example below), which states that the couple promises to do everything in their power to preserve the union.

So far, so good. Many people recommend premarital counseling to uncover expectations and beliefs and talk about them in a safe and open way with a neutral third party, and a 2006 study indicated a positive correlation between marital satisfaction, levels of commitment, and premarital counseling. It gets trickier, however, if a couple in a Covenant Marriage wants out, and, yes, even with a restrictive marriage license, there is still an out.

To get a divorce, there must be proof of abuse, addiction, infidelity, criminal behavior, or abandonment. If there was no wrongdoing,

A DECLARATION OF INTENT

We solemnly declare that marriage is a covenant between a man and a woman who agree to live together as husband and wife for as long as they both live. We have chosen each other carefully and have received premarital counseling on the nature, purposes, and responsibilities of marriage.

We understand that a Covenant Marriage is for life. If we experience marital difficulties, we commit ourselves to take all reasonable efforts to preserve our marriage, including marital counseling.

With full knowledge of what this commitment means, we do declare that our marriage will be bound by (Louisiana, Arizona, or Arkansas) law on Covenant Marriages, and we promise to love, honor, and care for one another as husband and wife for the rest of our lives.

couples have to wait two years, regardless of which of the three states they live in, before they can start the process.

Spaht and her husband, Paul, were among the first to convert their marriage. Spaht states she and Paul have been through many difficult life events in their nearly forty-three years of marriage, including her heart attack a few years back and her husband's cancer. "It's very powerful to renew vows after you've been through things like that together," Spaht says.

One of Spaht's sons and her daughter have also elected to get Covenant Marriages, so it's becoming a family affair, which is a source of pride for her.

Why such a small percentage of takers? We'll explain why in a minute. But first, let's look at who chooses it and why.

Penelope has been married for forty-three years. When the Louisiana resident learned about Covenant Marriage from her pastor fifteen years ago, she and her husband decided to convert. It's helped them get through tough spots.

"Covenant Marriage means that if you get to a place where you can't stand your spouse, you rethink your commitment and try harder to figure it out rather than just leave," she says, acknowledging that she'd been in that place a few times. "God has put us together and allowed bad things to happen, but God will also give you the strength to get through whatever the problem is."

Penelope shared with us how well it can work. A couple from her church was struggling because of the husband's womanizing and excessive drinking. Under the Covenant Marriage guidelines, the wife had legitimate grounds for a divorce, but rather than walk away, she decided to love her husband more, Penelope says. He eventually stopped drinking and "behaving badly," and he recommitted to the marriage. Knowing that he would have to go to counseling as well as answer to his pastor and their religious community, he sobered up to the fact that he had taken serious vows and he needed to honor them.

Of course, you don't have to be in a Covenant Marriage to get this outcome, but having the added accountability to a community makes it that much more challenging for couples to skip out without at least trying to work on the problems. That's the whole point. Penelope brings up God with good reason. Covenant Marriage was founded by religious conventionalists, and the majority of the couples that marry that way—about 78 percent—are conservative evangelical Protestants. While religion plays a role in Covenant Marriage, it's not exclusive to any religion in particular: there are Catholics, Quakers, and Jews in Covenant Marriages, as well as couples that identify with being spiritual rather than religious.

Two of the biggest proponents of Covenant Marriage don't even live in any of the states that offer it. Phil and Cindy Waugh live in Tennessee and started the Covenant Marriage Movement (CMM) in 1999 to help couples—primarily in the United States, but all over the world—prepare for and create Covenant Marriages. Phil Waugh is an ordained minister (although not affiliated with a particular church), and the work he and Cindy do has nothing to do with the legal side of marriage. The commitment they endorse is to the union, which he views as much more than committing to one another. "It's a commitment to God and to society as a whole. It's a way to contribute to the stability of the culture, and it's about putting the needs of others ahead of your own," he says.

The Waughs say they have helped hundreds of couples get in—and stay in—Covenant Marriages. They even have connections for assistance to spouses who, not through their own volition, have lost their Covenant partnership. (Yes, you can remain in your Covenant Marriage even if your spouse doesn't.) The Waughs regularly direct those individuals to the Oklahoma-based organization Covenant Keepers, which provides ongoing support to the spouse who has remained committed to the Covenant.

His organization is faith-based, but he says it's open to anyone—as long as the couple belongs to some sort of a community. The reason is accountability. Waugh says he has seen the huge benefits of answering to a larger group.

Brian and Stephanie went to the Waughs for their Covenant Marriage eleven years ago. They had learned about it from their friends. "Love is an action and not a feeling," the Florida couple told us. "You choose to keep loving your spouse even though there are times when you may not feel love toward the other."

And that's exactly what happened to them when they were displaced from their home because Brian changed his career path. As angry as Stephanie was at first, she realized her job was to find the solution within the marriage. That doesn't mean she didn't allow herself to experience the full depth of anger and sadness. Eventually, she mustered her strength and maturity—qualities she sees as vital in a Covenant Marriage—and accepted that their lives were going in a different direction, but not necessarily the wrong direction, than she had hoped. Rather than stay upset, Stephanie chose to trust their new situation and "love what is."

She, like others who have gone through the requirements of a Covenant Marriage, was taught in premarital counseling to make the best of difficult circumstances life throws your way and set your expectations accordingly. That's advice we support, too.

So, do Covenant Marriages actually prevent divorce? While they've done little to nothing to slow the general divorce rate in the three states that practice it, the divorce rate for couples with a Covenant Marriage is 50 percent lower than couples that have a plain old vanilla marriage license. This could be because those couples take their vows and commitment more seriously, or because they tend to be more religious and traditional, or because they are required to get premarital counseling, or all of the above or some combination.

Scott's parents had gone through a terrible divorce, and he wanted to avoid ever being in a situation that opened the door to such vitriol. When he saw a newspaper article about Covenant Marriage, he said to his then-girlfriend, Claudia, "If I get married, that's what I want to do."

Ten years after tying the knot, the Arizona couple is still happily married. They told us that the counseling they did before getting married was an integral part of building a lasting foundation, especially what they learned about conflict. "This helps guide us through the arguments and hard times that all married couples go through. We don't allow ourselves to live in a 'magic bubble' where we feel that we are special and bad things won't happen in our marriage. We feel it's important to realize that everyone fights, so we must fight fair in order to work through each issue as it comes up," they told us.

Even though the divorce rate is lower for couples in Covenant Marriages, some still divorce. Couples that live in states where Covenant Marriage is not legally recognized can simply go the traditional divorce route, but, in the three states where it's legal, it's more complicated.

If there are legitimate grounds that can be proven, such as physical or sexual abuse, felony criminal conviction, addiction, or abandonment, the spouse who wants out can get a divorce quickly. Proving the wrongdoing can be difficult, however, unless you're willing to hire private investigators or have witnesses. That can get really ugly really quickly, not to mention expensive. That's what made the courts move away from fault-based divorces in the first place. Couples that file without grounds must go through a two-year cooling-off period as we mentioned above to make sure they really want to split. They also must attend mandatory marriage therapy sessions to show that they made every attempt to keep the marriage intact.

To date, there is no information indicating that this waiting period has been effective in getting couples to reconcile, but given that the movement is relatively young and there are relatively few divorces in Covenant Marriages, perhaps it will prove a valuable tool.

There is a movement in America to make divorce harder for couples with minor children. But if the tiny number of those who choose to have a Covenant Marriage is any indication, it just won't fly. Two Arizona attorneys we spoke with, Victor Nirenstein and Alexander Garnice, believe they haven't caught on because "they are just too much hassle for most people."

Spaht and her cohorts believe differently. She says there's just too little knowledge about it. Policymakers pushed the measure through legislation, but little was done to oversee implementation of the program. She discovered clergy weren't telling their parishioners about it, and court clerks weren't handing out information on it even though they were mandated by state law to do so.

Covenant Marriage has received a great deal of criticism over the years. There are several reasons, including:

- Covenant Marriages are associated with the religious and political right, which many see as a narrow-minded population with rigid constraints. In fact, the majority of people today believe marital boundaries should widen rather than narrow.

- Covenant Marriage is defined solely between a man and a woman, so same-sex marriages are not recognized or encouraged.

- Premarital counseling is required, but few accommodations are made for couples that can't afford to pay for it.

- Emotional, mental, and verbal abuse are not considered grounds for divorce, although these can be as damaging as physical and sexual abuse.

- Misdemeanors are not considered grounds for divorce (just felonies are), so a spouse could be a low-level criminal, and the innocent spouse might still have to wait two years to divorce, opening him or her up to liability.

- The waiting period adds two years to the length of the marriage, which increases the amount of spousal support to be paid (however, if you are the one receiving the support, this may be a positive).

- Covenant Marriages are a throwback to a destructive model of divorce. People who have to prove fault are made to dredge up painful, embarrassing, and sometimes traumatizing events. Many consider fault-based divorces as shame-based.

Some have criticized Covenant Marriage as a dangerous step that could open the way for others to also redefine marriage and pave the way for multiple types of marriage, which naysayers believe will ultimately lead to privatizing marriage. But one of the main reasons we wrote this book is to acknowledge that people all over the world are already redefining marriage informally. The question wasn't *if* this was going to happen; it was just a matter of *when*.

We've never heard anyone complain that having more skills and knowledge about relationships has harmed their relationship. In fact, it seems glaringly obvious that couples that have only a few inter-relational skills to draw from fare worse than those with many skills. As is true with most things, the more you know, the better you do. But for the starry-eyed, mainstream marrier, counseling doesn't usually come up on the premarital list of things to do. According to one survey, just 39 percent sought professional help before they wed, and the vast majority of them (78 percent) found it helpful. And of the couples that didn't go for counseling, 76 percent said they wish they had.

One upside of getting premarital counseling is learning communication skills. One study found that Covenant couples are much less likely to use belittling, sarcastic, or hostile language—the kind of language that famed relationship expert John Gottman has found leads to poor marital quality.

Ironically, as we were writing this book, Colorado proposed the Colorado Marriage Education Act, mandating that all marrying couples complete ten hours of premarital education classes; those in second or third marriages would need more. Whether proposals like that pass or not, education for engaged couples might help decrease the number of divorces. It might also dissuade people from marrying when they're not ready to or from marrying the wrong person and ending up making what many consider "the biggest mistake of my life."

In this case, Covenant Marriages get it right. Another aspect of Covenant Marriage that seems to work well is the commitment spouses make to tell the other spouse when something in the relationship is not working. This is often what prompts couples to get marriage counseling. While a Covenant Marriage couple would likely go to counseling right away, those in traditional marriages usually wait to seek help until it's almost always too late—*six years* after problems arise.

Finally, even though Covenant Marriage makes things harder for a couple, it acknowledges that people should have the right to make whatever binding commitment they want to. Couples that enter a Covenant Marriage willingly give their lives over in service of their marriage and family, and they happily reject the notion of no-fault divorce.

IF YOU'RE ALREADY MARRIED

If you have a traditional marriage and you want to convert to a Covenant Marriage, you can, just like Penelope did. There are some hoops you must go through, however. In some cases, you may have to consult a trained professional to learn about the requirements and responsibilities, show proof that the original marriage ceremony took place, and pay an additional fee. You also must sign a modified Declaration of Intent stating that you understand the commitment you are making.

But before you do, please check your motives. If you have had a troubled marriage and hope a Covenant Marriage will force you or your spouse to be more committed or that it will magically solve some of your problems, think again. We would advise that you make sure your relationship is on solid ground for at least eighteen to twenty-four months before switching. Counseling may be more beneficial to your marriage than permanently tightening the reins would be. Using Covenant Marriage to manipulate your mate or to keep someone, even yourself, in check is not how the union was designed—and is generally not a healthy marital practice. As Stephanie cautioned earlier in the chapter, you need extra doses of fortitude and maturity to make this marriage work.

WHAT'S GOOD ABOUT A COVENANT MARRIAGE

- There is a higher level of commitment, so couples can have more confidence that the other will not leave. This may allow couples to go deeper with their love, trust, and intimacy.

- Since there is no easy exit, couples must work harder to get through difficult times and circumstances, and they may be more creative in solving their problems.

- Couples that participate in counseling before and during their marriage generally have better communication, conflict-reduction, and cooperation skills, as well as an overall increase in marital satisfaction.

- Covenant Marriages may provide more stability for children.

- Strong shared religious or traditional beliefs tend to unite a couple.

- Couples that choose this model embrace the concept of personal responsibility.

- Couples may feel support from their community.

- Covenant Marriages stress acceptance of the way things are, not how you'd like them to be.

- Covenant women become more optimistic about their marriages after they become mothers than do women in traditional marriages.

- Covenant women are less likely to envision divorce after they become mothers, whereas women in traditional marriages are more likely to envision divorce after the birth of a child.

- Covenant men become more optimistic about their marriages compared with men in traditional marriages.

WHAT'S NOT SO GOOD ABOUT
A COVENANT MARRIAGE

- Divorce, although more difficult to obtain, may still be necessary.

- It may carry some parochial expectations.

- It may perpetuate shame if a couple's marriage doesn't last.

- Covenant Marriage reinforces traditional gender roles.

- If one spouse causes the marriage to end, he or she may lose a community and support network in addition to a spouse.

- Others may judge you for having an "old-fashioned" and outdated marriage.

- A spouse may have a hidden agenda in asking you to agree to marry this way.

- You may have regrets.

- You may have a crisis in faith, which may change your desire to stay in a Covenant Marriage.

- Your spouse may have a crisis in faith, which may change his or her desire to stay in a Covenant Marriage.

- Your family may have to relocate, and your new home state may not legally recognize this marriage.

HOW TO MAKE A COVENANT MARRIAGE WORK

Given that this is already a legal model, a good amount of literature exists to help you structure your marriage. That said, it isn't a good model for everyone. The couples that tend to be attracted to it are religious and traditional (and, interestingly, more educated).

So, whom might it work for?

- You take commitment seriously.

- You want to be married for life and believe you can stay married.

- You don't see divorce as an option.

- You feel a social responsibility to marry and have children.

- You have a community to answer to.

- You have a certain level of maturity and strength.
- You are good at accepting "what is."
- You are flexible in seeking solutions.
- You are a good communicator.
- You have a good moral compass.
- You take responsibility for your behavior and actions.
- You are willing to sanctify your marriage.
- You believe in sticking with things no matter how challenging they are.
- You have a big-picture understanding of and a healthy respect for how your marriage impacts the world around you.

IS A COVENANT MARRIAGE RIGHT FOR ME?

Wondering if you're cut out for a Covenant Marriage? Here are a few questions you might want to ask yourself:

- What seems appealing about a Covenant Marriage?
- What seems negative?
- Why would I want to go through the extra hassles of a Covenant Marriage instead of just sticking to traditional marriage vows?
- Am I mature enough to deal with tremendous challenges in partnership without wanting an out?
- Are marriage and children central to my life?
- Are marriage and children central to my partner's life?
- Do I have a supportive community?
- In what ways do my religious or spiritual beliefs impact my relationships?
- In what ways am I traditional?
- In what ways am I nontraditional?
- How would I handle things if my spouse became unfaithful, abusive, an addict/alcoholic, or a felon?

- What are my feelings about divorce?
- What are my feelings about divorce with young children?
- Do I believe in monogamy, and am I good at monogamy?

READ MORE

Curious about how to make this marital model work? Here are some books to read for insight and guidance:

- *Covenant Marriage: Building Communication and Intimacy* by Gary Chapman (B&H Publishing Group, 2003).
- *Covenant Marriage: Staying Together for Life* by Fred Lowery (Howard Books, 2003).
- *Covenant Marriage: The Movement to Reclaim Tradition in America* by Steven Nock, Laura Sanchez, and James Wright (Rutgers University Press, 2008).
- *Covenant vs. Contract: Experiencing God's Blessing In and Through Your Marriage* by Dave Brown and Phil Waugh (Son Publishing, 2004).
- *Marriage Covenant* by Derek Prince (Whitaker House, 2006).

COVENANT MARRIAGE TAKEAWAYS

- Covenant Marriage is the only legal alternative to traditional marriage (but is only legal in Louisiana, Arizona, and Arkansas).
- Covenant Marriage is for life.
- Couples that choose Covenant Marriage must meet certain obligations, such as completing premarital counseling.
- Covenant Marriage requires a high level of maturity and emotional strength.
- There are only a few legitimate grounds for divorce in a Covenant Marriage (abuse, abandonment, addiction, and criminal involvement).
- If both spouses agree to divorce but there are no legal grounds for it, the couple must wait two years before they can get divorced.

Chapter 8

SAFETY MARRIAGE:

MONEY CAN BUY YOU
LOVE AND HAPPINESS

"I want a man who's kind and understanding.
Is that too much to ask of a millionaire?"
—Zsa Zsa Gabor

ill in the blank with the first word that comes to your mind:
Those who marry for money are _____.

While people from some cultures might respond with words like "wise," "prudent," or even "normal," if you are from a Western upbringing, your answer would probably not be nearly as kind and generous. Actually, we're pretty sure it would be negative, something along the lines of "gold-diggers," although "trophy wives," "leeches," "blood-suckers," and "sugar daddies" also come to mind. Regardless of the way you answered, the reality is that marrying for money is typically considered distasteful and inauthentic, and society harshly criticizes those who do it.

Case in point: Hugh Hefner and Crystal Harris. When the founder of Playboy married Harris, a model, on New Year's Eve 2012, few could overlook the sixty-year difference in age. He was eighty-six at the time and she was twenty-six. People didn't even bother to wonder what they could possibly have in common with that wide an age spread. It was obvious that their marriage was yet another typical younger-woman-gold-digger, older-man-sugar-daddy arrangement. There were a good share of Viagra jokes, and even Harris, a few months after they tied the knot, revealed that their most intimate moments are more about cuddling, watching movies, and playing board games than the kind of sexual antics Hefner has been known for since he started the Playboy empire decades ago.

It strained just about everyone's credibility that their marriage could be a "real" marriage. Yet, not every couple marries for love, children, or sex. In fact, couples marry for all sorts of reasons, including financial security and a desire to live in a lifestyle they're accustomed to or aspire to. That's what a Safety Marriage is all about.

A Safety Marriage is an agreement between two people, stated or not (but better if stated out loud and even better if stated in a prenup), that says, "You take care of me, and I'll take care of you." Sometimes the agreement is just, "I'll take care of you, and you owe me nothing," while other times the agreement is its flip side, "I have little to offer, but I need you to take care of me." More often, however, there is some sort of an equitable exchange: One spouse is financially secure—that does not always mean he or she is wealthy—and the other has something else to bring to the marital table, like sex, housekeeping, culinary skills, providing and raising children, or an ability to caretake. It can be an exchange of anything the couple agrees on, material or immaterial.

Harris openly admits that she married Hefner for security—not financial security, she says, but because she wanted to know that she was his one-and-only. And Hefner has made it clear that he loves her and wants to be with her for however long he's alive. Yes, there is a prenup, and Harris will be well taken care of when that day comes, but Hefner, who has four children from the first of his three marriages, did not include her in his will.

While it's all too easy to dismiss their marriage as less than a "real" marriage (and we'll explore the idea of a "real" marriage shortly), they are a couple that appears to have done marriage right—for them. They decided what they wanted, to trade one person's security for the other person's cozy companionship, and how to make it work. We consider that a successful marriage even if it's a marriage you may not want to have. Yet many cannot get past seeing the negative labels of their arrangement. What we find curious is that for a good part of society's not-so-distant past, women of Harris's age had no other choice *but* to marry so they could be financially supported, and no one would have considered them gold-diggers. Then again, there really weren't any good options for young women, which doomed women who didn't marry by a certain age—and at twenty-six, Harris would have been considered way, way past her prime—to a life of spinsterhood, toiling away at whatever low-paying job she could find or depending on the generosity of family. But if women married up, it was seen as a plus, and parents worked furiously behind-the-scenes to make sure their daughters married into proper (aka wealthy and prestigious) families. It was only after women became independent and could support themselves without needing to marry that "marrying up" was seen as distasteful.

A similar thing has happened to men. While men who marry women for money are also referred to as "gold-diggers" (or sometimes "gigolos"), they are often held in even higher contempt because of traditional expectations that males should be the primary breadwinners and providers. Not sure about that? Then please go back to the beginning of the chapter where we asked you to fill in the blank, and substitute the word "Those" with the word "Women." Then substitute "Those" with the word "Men." Did you notice having any more visceral disdain if it is a man being financially supported versus a woman? If so, it's an indication of how deeply ingrained the man-as-breadwinner stereotypes still remain in the collective psyche, despite the fact that more men are happily staying at home to raise the kids, and more women are either supporting their families or being an equal financial partner.

In any case, it's not really your fault that you think this way. You have most likely been unconsciously programmed by friends, family, media, Hollywood, and so-called experts to believe that marrying for financial reasons is wrong. But even those who took that belief to heart found out the hard way that it may not be such a bad idea as long as no one's being manipulated or hurt.

YOU DON'T KNOW WHAT YOU'VE GOT UNTIL IT'S GONE

Perhaps no one knows the importance of security more than those who do not have it. Just as marriage can bring a sense of safety, the end of a marriage can take it away.

Look at Terri Carlson. The forty-nine-year-old Southern California single mom of four kids lost her health insurance in a divorce. When her COBRA plan was close to running out, she began to look into her options. As it turns out, her options were slim to none. This was devastating news for Carlson, who was born with an autoimmune disease and would die without a certain pricey medication. There was no way she would be able to afford her medication without insurance, but, because hers was a pre-existing condition, she was repeatedly turned down (this was before President Obama's Affordable Care Act was launched).

Desperate for answers and help, she launched a blog with a name that both announced her dilemma and suggested a radical solution—Will Marry for Health Insurance. She had no idea if anyone would read it or even care about her situation, but, to her surprise, her plight struck a nerve. Pretty quickly, she got nearly 75,000 responses, including more than 38,000 marriage proposals, of which 12,000 were from military men. Why? People in the military earn significantly more money if they are married. The men who contacted her were well aware that they could benefit by helping someone they not only didn't love, but also didn't know. While some might judge Carlson for wanting to marry for the "wrong" reason, the military men who proposed to her were also viewing marriage through a narrow filter—as a financial boost. Honestly, neither view was far from marriage's origins. Marriage has always been about property, possessions, inheritance, and wealth (and in many ways, it still is).

Carlson managed to get health insurance through another avenue and so never ended up marrying any of her prospective suitors.

But her situation pulled at the heartstrings of many people. She was refreshingly open about the unconventional ways people can get what they need by marrying, like health insurance.

"Is there ever a good reason to get married other than for love? Yeah, life and death," she says. "There are people who are literally losing their life. They have no health insurance. They're going to lose their home. They're going to lose their life savings. In situations like that, when you're talking life and death, yeah, you would marry to save your life and get the treatment that you need."

Carlson estimates that only about 5 percent of those who contacted her were men looking to offer her a marriage proposal. The rest were women in similar situations (stay-at-home-moms who were ineligible for disability and who were getting divorced), or they were women who had jobs but lost them in the Great Recession. Some had already married to be protected; others were looking to marry, too. They were grateful to Carlson for making the need to marry for insurance so public. Many of the correspondents even asked Carlson to send her rejects their way.

What about you? Would you tie the knot if you thought it was your only option? Do you judge people who see marriage as a way to solve a problem as Carlson did, whether an immediate or long-term need? If your good friend was struggling and looking for a partner who could help her care for her kids, financially and emotionally, would you judge her or try to talk her out of it? Would you feel differently if your friend were a struggling single, widowed, or divorced dad? If your friend, regardless of gender, found someone who was willing to get hitched and take on that role, would that change your perception? If you were the one struggling or the one who was financially secure, would your opinion change?

A comment we received from a woman who'd married for financial security, among other reasons, beautifully illustrates the benefit of a Safety Marriage: "My husband and I are like the odd couple. I'm business and classy, he is a lumberjack motorcycle-riding country boy. But it works. I married for financial security, safety, and sex. My husband makes me feel safe. I know he would fight Satan himself to keep me safe. I fell in love with him because he promised to always be there. And he has."

She's not alone in her thinking. Many would be happy to marry just like she did if the opportunity presented itself. According to a 2007 survey by Connecticut-based Prince & Associates, two-thirds of the women and half of the men polled indicated they would be "very" or "extremely" willing to tie the knot for money. How much? An average of $1.5 million. Who was most willing? Women in their thirties (74 percent) and men in their forties (61 percent), causing even those who study such things to be somewhat rattled. "It's kind of against the notion of love and soul mates and the main motivations to marry in our culture," says sociologist Pamela Smock, whose own studies reveal that couples are more likely to marry if they have money and if the husband-to-be is economically stable.

Another study by evolutionary psychologists David Buss and Todd Shackelford found similar results. They looked at what attractive women want in a mate, and what they discovered is that good-looking women want—and presumably would be able to get, by virtue of their looks alone—it all. Beyond wanting a man who's handsome, smart, and has a desire for a family, they also wanted a man who is a few years older (and thus likely to be earning more than a younger man) with high-income potential and "earning capacity."

These studies tell us that many women view their husband's financial potential as a sort of backup plan; maybe they hope to have kids one day and want a financially stable partner so they can take time off from their career to stay home. As we mentioned in the Parenting Chapter, Beyoncé and Jay-Z placed a monetary value on that in the event they divorced—$5 million per child. Or maybe they want to go back to college for an advanced degree, launch a business, or pursue an artistic endeavor and need their partner to pay the bills during that time.

We don't doubt that there are some men nowadays who scrutinize a woman's financial situation just as carefully. And they should. There are many men who would be wary of marrying a woman with a massive student loan or credit card debt, and rightfully so. But while many women marry believing they will have options they didn't have as a singleton—whether quitting a job, working part time, or continuing to work full time—most men don't wed with the same expectations. And while many women grow up hearing, "It's just as easy to fall in love with a rich guy as it is to fall in love with a poor one," we can't imagine many parents encouraging a son to "marry up"—even in this presumably enlightened age.

Maybe part of the problem is that humans are not as enlightened as we think we are. For the most part, many men and women are still stuck in traditional gender models, especially when it comes to a husband's financial role. Many people still believe that a husband should make more money than his wife. The couples in which the wife earns more than her husband surprisingly "report being less happy, report greater strife in their marriage, and are ultimately more likely to get a divorce."

That does not bode well for husbands who might want to be supported for staying home to raise the kids, or for women who thrive at busting through corporate glass ceilings. The way couples often work around it is by having the wife work part time or drop out of the workforce for a while (typically for raising the kids). Wives also tend to take on more of the housekeeping so their high-income potential appears less threatening to their husband. Again, these are hardly satisfying answers for more egalitarian-minded couples that hope to break through gendered marital stereotypes. And they reinforce unhealthy power dynamics when one spouse has more money, therefore more power, than the other.

As much as money can be a divisive issue for couples, it can also be a unifier. Not long ago we asked a couple that had been in a longtime loving and committed cohabiting relationship why they eventually tied the knot. Without skipping a beat, they said, "For the tax perks." That's why Betsy and Warren Talbot, whom you met in the chapter on Companionship Marriage, got married. We wonder why no one would question a couple that stays married for financial reasons, but everyone looks down on a single man or woman who wants to get hitched for the same reason—money. It doesn't make sense.

CAN MONEY COME FIRST?

According to the Pew Research Center, marrying for financial stability trails behind marrying for love, making a lifelong commitment, companionship, and having children. Now, imagine if the
same study revealed that financial stability was the number one
reason to tie the knot—how would people react? More important,
how would *you* react?

We are perplexed why so many people—perhaps even you—
believe that it's okay for financial security to be *among* the top reasons to get hitched, but not *the* main reason. What does that reveal
about society? Does a strong desire for financial security make people
appear shallow—the same as if they have a preference for attractive,
slender, and younger mates? What would be the financial break-off
point that would make a marriage "suspect"? If a woman married a
man who earned $80,000 a year, would she be seen as a gold-digger?
What if the man made $300,000 a year? What about $1 million or
$10 million? Would her age matter? Would his age matter? Would her
age matter more if he were worth more? Would it make a difference
if the one with the money were a woman? Would it make a difference
if the couple were a same-sex couple? (And we're pretty sure there is
gold-digging in same-sex relationships, too.)

The fact is everyone needs money, and there's nothing wrong in
stating that openly. But why would it matter if someone's desire for
financial security meant marrying with the goal of having enough
cash to live the so-called American Dream versus someone who marries to have a more lavish lifestyle? Why is it considered "wrong" to
marry with a desire to live comfortably? Your view on how much
financial security matters probably depends a lot on your background
and education level. People without a college education are more
likely to see financial security as the main reason to get married; in
fact, nearly four times as many noncollege graduates as college graduates say "financial security is the main benefit of marriage."

Ironically, the people who are among the most pragmatic about
marriage and its financial ramifications are the ones who aren't marrying at all—those at the lowest socioeconomic levels. Studies have

shown that, although they value marriage and have more traditional views about marriage and divorce than others, financial concerns are among the reasons that prevent them from getting hitched.

A partner who isn't contributing financially is a handicap, as one young single mother says in Kathryn Edin and Maria Kefalas's groundbreaking book, *Promises I Can Keep: Why Poor Women Put Motherhood Before Marriage:* "I started thinking, 'I don't need him.' He was just like an extra burden. It was actually easier without him."

Since research indicates that couples fight more about money than about issues like sex, chores, or kids, it's obvious that money matters a lot when it comes to marriage. Why not be upfront and honest about that, especially if you want to make it the number one reason to marry? One high-end matchmaker told us that she had successfully found husbands for a handful of her female clients who were looking to marry for money as a top priority. We weren't all that surprised that none would talk with us even though we guaranteed them anonymity. Why? Because there is a lot of societal judgment, shame, and misunderstanding around those sorts of marriages.

Melissa Chapman knows that all too well. Still, she has no qualms about admitting that she married for money fourteen or so years ago. Her website, MarriedMySugarDaddy.com, pretty much says it all. Chapman acknowledges that many people might see her as a "money-grubbing whore" (her words), but she says anyone who views her that way would be missing the point. "What self-respecting women in her thirties would actually ADMIT to marrying a sugar daddy? . . . Anyone who has married knows there are so many factors that go into the decision you make when you meet The One. And sure, when I met 'my one,' he happened to be fifteen years older than me and a well-established physician. But to say that I was looking for a bank account rather than a husband—while that may appear to be the method behind my madness—it is oh so much more complicated than that."

The New York woman adds she was groomed by her family to marry a medical doctor for a secure, luxurious life. Although she wished she heard more positive financial messages, like maybe she should boost her own income by getting an advanced degree, she went with the program. She admits there have been times that issues surrounding money almost busted apart her marriage, but she says money isn't the problem per se—it's how a couple *communicates* about the money they have or don't.

"Two people will never enter a marriage completely on equal footing in regards to finances, and throughout the course of a relationship, financial circumstances will ebb and flow. The important thing is to keep talking and sharing and remembering that money, and how you handle it and whose responsibility it is, all comes down to how you talk to one another."

We agree with her. Couples need to be on the same page about their finances. Many aren't. In fact, a third of American couples admit to financial infidelity, such as hiding bank accounts, cash, debt, or earnings, according to a 2011 Harris poll.

It's not enough to assume you're financially stable even if you're in a Safety Marriage because financial situations can change drastically.

A LESSON FROM THE ECONOMIC MELTDOWN

In the first decade of the twenty-first century, those living in the Western world saw an unprecedented number of social norms change when their financial security evaporated. People lost homes, income, jobs, savings, and benefits. Many had no choice but to modify their lifestyles and find creative solutions to problems caused by the down economy. The Great Recession, which hit in 2007 and continued through 2009 with lingering repercussions, was a startling reminder for people around the world that financial safety is not something to be taken for granted. Couples that may have wanted to tie the knot decided to put off the wedding until they knew they could afford it; wannabe parents postponed having children until the fiscal climate was stronger; and many unhappy couples either had to stay together or, in some cases, move back in together, in order to avoid financial ruin.

During the worst of the housing crisis, Susan realized that nearly one-fifth of her clients were homeless, including an attorney, an accountant, and a therapist. Not the typical people you expect to find homeless, but the economic downturn was an equal-opportunity destroyer. Of the handful of homeless divorcées she worked with, one went from being down and out—husbandless, jobless, and penniless (all the while mortified because she had to move in with her aging parents)—to engaging in a full-fledged pursuit of her next mate. Once she got over her initial grief of losing her husband, she started dating like crazy and was focused on finding a man who could provide for her. Within six months, she had a new home, a part-time job, and a new last name with, of course, a brand-new set of purse strings. Only those who knew her situation understood what happened and why. The rest of the world congratulated her as the lucky new Mrs. Jones.

The stories from Susan's client and Terri Carlson highlight how quickly a person's financial situation can change, and how desperate times sometimes lead to desperate measures. The popularity of websites like SugarDaddyForMe.com and Sugardaddie.com, which aren't sites where most singles would go to specifically look for mates, casts a harsh light on what people are willing to do for financial security. SeekingArrangement.com, a popular site for college students and single mothers for its cash-for-services approach, says it sees increased membership during economically trying times. It experienced a huge spike in enrollment during the government shutdown in fall 2013.

Money talks when it comes to dating, love, and marriage.

IS MARRYING FOR MONEY SMART?

Gabriela married twice for love. Never again, she told us. After her second husband cheated on her—"the heartbreak of my life"—all she wanted to do was date and have fun. Two years later, she met Ramon, who flipped for her. "I kept telling him I did not want a husband; just a fun lover," she told us. So, of course, he proposed.

A professional childfree woman in the Midwest with a satisfying and stable career of her own, Gabriela eventually gave in; she was close to fifty and realized it would be nice to have a companion and a little more security. "We even joke that he married me for sex and I married him for money. He's also financially independent, but more independent than me, if you know what I mean. He knows how I feel about this silly love thing. I often tell him I *like* him very much, which makes him very happy, as he knows I really mean it. I don't go around just saying, 'I love you' like many couples, who don't really feel the importance of the words," she says. "The second husband kept saying he loved me, even after I found out he was having an affair. Honestly, if that is love, I don't need it!"

She believes that marrying for security and companionship is a much better deal than marrying for love, especially for women. "Love gets in the way of true happiness, I feel. It blinds you. It makes you vulnerable and weak."

Two women who would likely agree with Chapman are Elizabeth Ford and Daniela Drake, authors of *Smart Girls Marry Money: How Women Are Getting Shafted by their Romantic Expectations—and What They Can Do About It.* The two Los Angeles divorcées say they "married for love, but reaped the consequences." They say they wrote their book to help other women avoid their fate:

> Find your fortune while you're young and marry a man with money. This is what we call the Gold-Digging Imperative—"The GDI."
>
> We don't think "gold-digging" should be frowned upon. Why, we wonder, does society applaud a girl who falls for a guy's big blue eyes yet denounces one who chooses a man with a big green bankroll?
>
> What's the difference? Earning power is, after all, a reflection of his values and character. Big blue eyes? Not so much . . . It's time to start treating your life like reality, not a fairy tale. We live in a world that runs on dollars and good sense. The GDI can prevent a future that no smart girl believes will happen to her.

While their satirical take on things might seem a bit too harsh for some women (and may scare men who might believe *all* women feel this way), the bigger message is an important one—that couples must be able to talk about money, how they feel about it, what they use it for, and whether they have a financial plan for the future.

That's what Ginger Borgella insists women do on her popular blog Girls Just Want to Have Funds. In her mind, the way a man honors his debts and obligations is an indication of how he will treat his wife. When the thirty-four-year-old Maryland therapist married in 2006, she insisted on seeing her potential husband's credit report first. (It wasn't all that good, but they agreed to a course of action to create financial security for both of them.)

Financially savvy women need to understand money and have a financial plan of action for themselves first, she advises. They also need to pay attention to how a potential mate spends his dough, especially since a recent survey indicates that married men overwhelmingly are the ones wearing the pants when it comes to making household financial and investment decisions.

Is there an emergency fund? Are bills paid on time? Do expenses exceed earnings? Is money seen as a tool or a crutch? Is there a financial plan for the future? Do you both share the same values when it comes to money?

Understanding money, realizing its potential, acknowledging that few can survive very well without it, and choosing a mate who feels the same way as you do is not the same as gold-digging. It's a Safety Marriage.

Who hasn't heard the expression, "Money can't buy happiness"? How often have you heard that the best things in life are free? Hogwash, says Harvard psychology professor Daniel Gilbert, author of *Stumbling on Happiness*. Money *does* buy happiness—enough money, that is. He believes $50,000 to $75,000 a year should do it. But having more than that only makes people marginally more happy, he says, in part because wealthier people don't always spend their money in truly satisfying ways. Not everyone needs to be a millionaire, but, when people have enough to cover bills, go on vacations, and financially support the causes they believe in, they are generally happier people.

We are not advocating that you marry someone just for his or her portfolio or income potential. We would not be able to support you if you intended to marry with a hidden financial agenda. If you plan to quit work and stay home with your future unborn children but haven't discussed that with your spouse-to-be, or if you have always wanted to start a business and view your potential spouse as a "bank," or if you have been hiding debt from him or her, you are being deceptive. A marriage that begins on false premises is doomed. Our definition of marrying for financial security means you and your partner have similar values and goals when it comes to money, and you both agree to a plan of action. If both of you are willing participants and go into a marriage with your eyes wide open, your plan of action really isn't anyone else's business. It's a private arrangement.

And, to be clear, we are not discounting that you probably have other reasons you may want to tie the knot. Just because financial security is the most important goal for you doesn't mean that you don't value such things as companionship, love, and commitment. That said, while you might not want to have a marital arrangement like Hefner and Harris's, and while we might not want to have it either, we are 100 percent supportive of couples that marry despite a huge age gap and a huge monetary gap as long as it's a mutually happy decision.

Many people roll their eyes at May-December marriages and insist that those are not "real" marriages. Which leads us to ask, well, just what is a "real" marriage? One in which the couple is close in age or the same age? One in which the couple is on the same economic footing? One in which the couple has the same goals? One in which the couple desires to make a public and legal commitment? One that is solely to have kids? All of the above?

When you come down to it, all that matters is that the arrangement is mutually agreed to, the couple is happy with their lifestyle, and that neither is being deceived, manipulated, or in any way hurt or disadvantaged. If people were more willing to embrace the idea of marrying for financial security, no one who did so would have to suffer judgment or have his or her marriage questioned as a "real" marriage.

MARRIAGE, INC.

We'd like you to think of marriage as a business contract—because it is, as you saw in Chapter 3. It's easy to forget that when you are going about your day-to-day marital business, but it will be a painful reality slap in the face if you end up divorced. No family court judge or divorce lawyer or mediator will care much if at all about who loved whom more, who was more committed, who worked harder on the job or at home, or who messed up more. All that matters is how you plan to split your possessions and finances, and, if you have children, how you will handle custody. It's not very romantic.

Marriage is indeed just like any other business (notice we said *like* a business; it obviously has many more emotional and cultural meanings than if you opened up an organic frozen yogurt shop). Despite the fact that people freely use terms such as "marriage contract," and "divorce court," many still don't seem to understand that marriage is at its heart a business deal. So if you want to get married, looking at the financial part of the equation is not only smart but also essential.

REINVENTING YOUR EXISTING MARRIAGE

Remember Betsy and Warren Talbot of Married With Luggage? Although they were a committed, loving couple before they wed, they openly admit that they tied the knot for the tax perks. Both had big-income corporate careers and all the trappings that go along with that lifestyle. Money and consumption were integral parts of their marriage, and they had the debt to prove it.

When that became less and less satisfying, they realized that in order to transform their marriage from one rich in possessions into one rich in experiences, they would again need to turn to their old friend, money, but in a different way. They set a budget and a deadline, and then paid off their debt, pinched pennies, sold stuff, and saved until they had enough to live their dream of traveling the world.

You and your spouse may not want to travel the world, but you probably have other goals, perhaps a desire to have a baby. There is no stronger pull on your need for financial safety and no greater change to the terms of your marriage contract than when you become parents. Whether you like it or not, when you have kids, you have to redefine your relationship with each other as well as the fiscal terms of your marriage. But far too many couples go into parenthood with only vague ideas of how to plan for it financially, and we don't mean buying the crib, stroller, and car seat.

While our chapter on a Parenting Marriage addresses the nuts and bolts of what needs to be in place before a baby is born—clarity on education, religion, how many children and timing, parenting styles, discipline, medical decisions such as circumcision and vaccinations, etc.—the shift in power if a dual-income partnership becomes a single-income partnership is challenging. This is when you will need to have a mutual plan of action with agreements on budgeting, savings, and at what point the stay-at-home parent returns to employment, if at all. The discussion must include a clear understanding of who does which tasks so there are no assumptions that the stay-at-home person is responsible for handling all the childcare and housework. That's what leads many at-home parents to frustration and resentment. A Safety Marriage with an at-home parent is a "you take care of me, and I'll take care of you" arrangement, with very defined, mutually agreed upon, and respected responsibilities.

Sometimes, spouses may have to shift their arrangement when something unforeseen occurs to the provider—a long-term illness, a job loss, or a disability. Not only will the other spouse have to become a physical caretaker, but he or she also may have to become a financial caretaker, which may mean a return to the workforce, adding extra hours to an existing job, or taking on a second job. Many wives—perhaps as many as 2 million—had to do just that at the height of the economic downturn.

The word "mancession" was coined because so many men lost their jobs. Joblessness and economic instability often wreak havoc on a couple's marital happiness. Some couples have yet to fully recover. Rather than wait until a time of crisis, you might want to have a plan of action "just in case" so you can be on the same page about who will do what.

Another unforeseen change to a couple's monetary reality may be more positive but could create problems nonetheless—if the spouse being provided for receives a financial windfall, such as an unexpected inheritance or a part-time hobby that turns into a successful business venture. Anything that suddenly puts a couple on more equal financial footing could create a fracture in their marriage, as their dynamic would change. This is when a couple would have to renegotiate their arrangement.

Whether you're thinking about getting married or renegotiating your existing marriage, we can't stress enough how important it is to voice your requisites when it comes to money, especially around feeling financially secure. Disagreements about finances can be upsetting not simply because money provides a sense of safety but because money also represents love, power, self-esteem, control, and freedom. A 2011 study about mates and money found that couples that fight once a week about money are twice as likely to divorce than those who have disagreements fewer than once a month. Talking openly and honestly about finances can make a big difference in resolving conflicts. Having matching financial goals and expectations can determine whether you stay married or not.

WHAT'S GOOD ABOUT A SAFETY MARRIAGE

- It may help you get more of your and your spouse's needs met.
- You may feel less vulnerable.
- You and your spouse's expectations and values will be aligned.
- You and your spouse will share the same financial goals.
- Financial security may lead to higher marital satisfaction.
- You will have a stronger foundation than if you married for love.
- It offers better potential to create the life you want.
- You will be better prepared financially for crises.

- You will be better prepared financially for children.

- You may have fewer arguments over money.

- You will be better equipped to adjust your marital arrangement as your life situation changes.

- There will be no hidden financial surprises such as excess debt.

- You will have a safety net.

- Spouses may have more flexibility in choosing different paths, such as switching careers, continuing education, or pursuing new business ventures or passions.

- You may feel great pleasure and pride in your role as giver/receiver.

- You will likely be better prepared for retirement.

- You may feel empowered.

- You may be better able to address typical gendered divisions of labor.

WHAT'S NOT SO GOOD ABOUT A SAFETY MARRIAGE

- You may be tempted to misuse your situation.

- You might face judgment and misunderstanding from other people.

- Financial situations change, which may lead to marital dissatisfaction or divorce.

- It might create a power imbalance.

- It could create a feeling of entitlement.

- It could lead to resentments.

- It could lead to trust issues.

- A spouse may have a change of heart.

- You may have regrets.

- You may feel that you "sold out."

- You may have a false sense of security.

- You may feel disempowered and controlled.

- You may be unhappy with a gendered division of labor.

HOW TO MAKE A SAFETY MARRIAGE WORK

When done well—meaning both of you are open about the agreements you're entering into—a Safety Marriage works well and can make you feel truly empowered. However, if transparency and full disclosure are not part of the equation regarding the terms of the relationship, one or both of you may feel exploited. That can be extremely demeaning; no one likes to feel used. We can't emphasize enough the need to enter into this marriage with mutual agreement and respect.

This marriage may be successful if:

- You are okay with ignoring or gently responding to how others perceive your marriage.
- It doesn't bother you if others judge you.
- You are clear about your needs—whether it's to be provider or provided for—and are able to communicate that.
- You appreciate what each of you bring into the relationship and see it as equal.
- You share the same financial mind-set and goals.
- You share the same lifestyle goals.
- You are comfortable talking about money.
- You can make clear agreements and stick to them.
- You value stability over risk.
- You are able to see marriage as a business arrangement.
- You have a healthy relationship to money.
- You don't take advantage of people or situations.
- Your identity isn't tied to your financial situation.

IS A SAFETY MARRIAGE RIGHT FOR ME?

. . . .

Wondering if you're cut out for a Safety Marriage? Here are a few questions you might want to ask yourself:

- What are my reasons for choosing a Safety Marriage?
- Am I comfortable with how much money I make on my own?
- What prevents me from making more?
- What does money mean to me?
- What experiences in my past led me to feel that way?
- Do I trust myself with money?
- In what ways do I have a healthy relationship with money?
- What are my spending habits?
- What are my saving habits?
- In what ways do I see money as status?
- Is it easy for me to share?
- Am I able to talk openly and honestly about money?
- Do I sometimes hide purchases from a partner?
- What are my short-term financial goals?
- What are my long-term financial goals?
- In what way do I want to be taken care of?
- In what way do I want to take care of someone else?
- What would I do differently if I had more money?
- Do I believe the best things in life are free?
- Do I believe money can buy happiness?
- What financial decisions have I regretted?
- Do my partner and I respect and respond to each other's needs and wants?
- Do my partner and I have the same financial values?

READ MORE

Curious about how to make this marital model work? Here are some books to read for insight and guidance:

- *Emotional Currency: A Woman's Guide to Building a Healthy Relationship with Money* by Kate Levinson (Celestial Arts, 2011).
- *Financial Infidelity* by Bonnie Eaker Weil (Plume, 2008).
- *First Comes Love, Then Comes Money: A Couple's Guide to Financial Communication* by Bethany Palmer and Scott Palmer (HarperOne, 2009).
- *Get Financially Naked: How to Talk Money with Your Honey* by Manisha Thakor and Sharon Kedar (Adams Media, 2009).
- *How to Marry Money* by Kevin Doyle (Plume, 2004).
- *Money Harmony: Resolving Money Conflicts in Your Life and Relationships* by Olivia Mellan (Walker & Company, 1995).
- *On My Own Two Feet: A Modern Girl's Guide to Personal Finance* by Manisha Thakor and Sharon Kedar (Adams Business, 2007).
- *Prenup/Postnup: How They Work and Why You Might Need One* by Richard G. Kent (BookSurge Publishing, 2009).
- *Prenups for Lovers: A Romantic Guide to Prenuptial Agreements* by Arlene Dubin (Villard, 2001).
- *Smart Couples Finish Rich: 9 Steps to Creating a Rich Future for You and Your Partner* by David Bach (Crown Business, 2002).
- *Smart Girls Marry Money: How Women Have Been Duped into the Romantic Dream—And How They're Paying for It* by Elizabeth Ford and Daniela Drake, M.D., (Running Press Book Publishers, 2010).
- *What to Do Before I Do: The Modern Couple's Guide to Marriage, Money, and Prenups* by Nihara Choudhri (Sphinx Publishing, 2004).

SAFETY MARRIAGE TAKEAWAYS

- Marriage is a legal contract, and it's important to see it as a business negotiation. That's what a Safety Marriage does.

- A Safety Marriage provides each spouse with a sense of safety and well-being. The quid pro quo approach is overt and talked about openly.

- A Safety Marriage puts the need for financial and even emotional security on par with (and perhaps even higher than) love as the reason to marry.

- A Safety Marriage can provide status as well.

- Ignoring money matters in a partnership is a recipe for disaster.

- For many cultures around the world, financial security remains the sole reason to marry.

Chapter 9

OPEN MARRIAGE:

WHY MONOGAMY?

"Monogamy is a way of getting the versions
of ourselves down to the minimum."
—Adam Phillips

*B*ryce readily admits that he isn't cut out for monogamy. When he met Dana, he was thrilled that she was open to inviting another lover into their bed. While they were dating, this couple in their thirties had threesomes, and they even swapped partners on their wedding night six years ago.

In their first two years of marriage, the Pennsylvania couple had sex with others together. Then they talked about having sex with others separately. They felt like they were in a good place, that they trusted each other, and had confidence to explore. But like many others in open relationships, they had rules—the sex was always safe, there were no sleepovers, and every arrangement was to be agreed to beforehand.

Their extramarital romps are just about sex, period; they're not looking to forge relationships and explore deeper intimacy with others. They admit it's a lot easier for Dana to have men believe her when she says she's in an open marriage. "The general consensus is, well, this girl wants to have sex, she's attractive, and she's married, and she doesn't want me to be her boyfriend. Guys really go for that," Dana says with a laugh.

While they set up their marriage to be open, they've only put it into action a handful of times since they tied the knot. "[Because of] the fact we have the freedom to do it, it's not as big of a drive," Bryce says. "If I were not allowed, that would be worse."

Their goal is to recognize and celebrate each other's needs. "We want each other to be happy, and we know sometimes either one of us might want to have a sexual experience with somebody else that would make us happy. For me, that's what it's all about," Dana says.

What about you? Where would you draw the line on celebrating your partner's sexual needs and happiness—or your own? Most people don't question whether they're really suited for monogamy or not, as Bryce and Dana have. Even though people today are growing up in more diverse families than ever before and are much more open to and accepting of broader views of gender and sexuality than generations past, society still tends to view non-monogamous relationships negatively. Just look at the language that's used to talk about it. Those who engage in it are either promiscuous, putting themselves and others at risk of sexually transmitted diseases, or cheaters, with a breakup being the expected outcome once an affair is discovered. It's all about diseases, betrayal, secrecy, and deception. The way most people view non-monogamy focuses on everything wrong about it. Instead of seeing it as a new way to be a couple, and perhaps a healthier way, it's seen as "a libertarian, individualistic, hedonistic pursuit of sexual variety."

There are scant positive models of healthy non-monogamous relationships, and so monogamy is generally not considered a choice but a given. Once a couple commits to each other, sexual exclusivity is expected and assumed—for now and forever.

Is that a reasonable expectation? Is monogamy willingly embraced or just endured? Most people believe a healthy sex life is important in a marriage—70 percent, according to a Pew survey. Most couples start off their newlywed life by having sex whenever and wherever they can. Then it slows down a bit, usually in the second or third year, and, if kids come along, it often sputters and slows—if it even happens at all. Frustration and resentment become uneasy marital-bed partners.

Sex, or rather the lack of it, is one of the major complaints for longtime couples. Let's face it; the stuff of daily living tears away at what many consider essential to happy, healthy relationships—feeling desired and desirable. That's tough to maintain, and, if you don't believe us, look at what's being promoted in most women's and men's magazines: "Hot Sex Trends Worth Trying," "10 New Sex Positions You've Never Heard of . . . But Need to Try, Now," "5 Sex Moves You Think She Likes, But Doesn't," and "The Couple's Toy You Need to Try." There are few options presented to couples other than adding sexual novelty—new positions, sex toys, lingerie, maybe watching soft-core porn together—to their repertoire.

Enter infidelity. For the cheating partner, affairs can be exhilarating; for the cuckolded partner, however, affairs are anything but. Instead, they can be devastating. Affairs often lead straight to divorce, but sometimes couples try to salvage their marriage, typically through marital counseling. As they sit uncomfortably in a counselor's office, someone—the straying wife or husband—will likely be labeled the "bad" one. A good therapist might approach the idea that they both have a certain responsibility in creating the dynamics that led to the affair—if it takes two to make a good relationship, it takes two to make a dysfunctional one, even if it's not fifty-fifty or sixty-forty or even eighty-twenty. But what do you think the chances are that the counselor will disclose that the unhappy couple isn't the only couple struggling with infidelity, that a huge percentage of his or her clients as well as the clients of other counselors are seeking help for the same problem? Zip.

Infidelity isn't just a couple's problem; it's a societal problem. A big one. Why aren't more people talking about what might be behind all that desire to fool around? As much as people say they are for fidelity—and 93 percent say they believe being faithful is the key to a successful marriage—many don't actually live up to their own ideals.

Studies indicate that infidelity rates may be as high as 60 percent to 70 percent, although others believe 25 percent might be a more realistic number.

Even if the low-end numbers are accurate, that means that one in four couples still deals with some type of breach to their exclusive coupledom. That may be because, as social scientists have discovered, monogamy is a function of evolution believed to be for the well-being of children. But sticking around to help raise the kids and being faithful to one mate, and only one mate, are really different. Viewing infidelity (particularly with men) in the light of "a natural inclination" can definitely ease the pathological slant we put on straying. Unless, of course, it's *your* husband we're talking about.

Regardless of the science behind monogamy or the statistics, let's get back to how this affects you personally. Take a look at the couples you know for a better gauge. How many of your friends have cheated or been cheated upon? How many have experienced a parent's infidelity? What's your own infidelity story? We know countless people who have borne the burden of infidelity and either saw their marriage fall apart because of it or somehow found a way to work past it and stay together. What do you think the high percentage of married people who fool around on the side says about fidelity in marriage and monogamy in general? To us, it says many people, despite their best intentions to be faithful, despite their vows to be true, despite their upbringing or steadfast belief that they would never, ever want to hurt their loved one by acting on a desire for someone else, struggle with monogamy.

We think if more of us admitted openly and loudly that we struggle with monogamy, there would be less pain—whether from acting on desires or not acting on desires—and less shame surrounding the entire issue. So, where does that leave you? We hope that you'll start by having a discussion about monogamy—with yourself. Are you a monogamous person by nature (and please reflect on your behavior and actions in past relationships), or are you monogamous because you've bought into the cultural norm? Monogamy is a choice, despite everyone's assumption that it's some sort of social mandate. Then when you're clear on how you feel about monogamy—or even if you're still somewhat fuzzy about where you stand—we hope you would be able to discuss it openly, honestly, and lovingly with your partner.

Admittedly, it's a hard conversation. Being honest about such things as desire, fidelity, and sexual needs tend to be delicate and challenging. So rather than address monogamy directly and compassionately, people tend to not bring it up at all. It's a quick-fix way to deal with—actually, to avoid—the issue. Not for everyone, however. Gay men generally tend to negotiate the "tension between desire and domesticity more creatively and honestly than mainstream heterosexual culture encourages people to do," notes *Unhitched: Love, Marriage, and Family Values from West Hollywood to Western China* author Judith Stacey.

That's not to say that all gay men have open relationships, and the ones who do not are understandably loath to be thrown into a stereotype. But a certain percentage have what author and syndicated sex-advice columnist Dan Savage calls a "monogamish" arrangement—they tend to be monogamous, but dalliances are okay at certain times with certain agreed-upon conditions. What should matter more than fidelity, says Savage, who has been monogamishly married since 2012, is the deep connection, intimacy, and history a couple has after being together for a long time. Not the occasional quickie. And, let's not forget that there are lots of ways to "cheat" on your partner without actually having sex with someone else. Indifference, emotional neglect, refusing to be intimate, denying sex, contempt—they are just as damaging, and maybe more, in the long run as a spouse's one-night stand.

Like Stacey, Savage, and many others, we believe couples should place a higher value on marital stability than on marital monogamy. What matters most to you—stability or monogamy? Okay, we get it; you probably want both. Yet if you had to put them in descending order according to importance, what would you say? How might your choice differ if you had young children? It's an uneasy choice, but a real choice nonetheless.

We don't outright embrace the idea of an occasional affair as a healthy marital model as Savage does. Affairs can be destructive even if they are few and far between. What we absolutely embrace, however, is that you and your partner have open and frank discussions about consensual non-monogamy, which includes a vast array of arrangements, from open relationships to swinging to long-term commitments with sexual and emotional attachments to multiple partners to sex-only relationships. It isn't as rare as you may think—somewhere between 4.3 percent to 10.5 percent of all relationships identify that way, and we believe many more have experimented with it at one point or another. It's just that people aren't always open about their sex life, especially since non-monogamy is viewed so negatively, so it's hard to have a good grasp on the numbers.

As broad-minded as those who seek alternative romantic relationships may appear to be, there isn't one flavor of consensual non-monogamy. Some are happy swinging at private parties; others head to resorts that cater to those "in the lifestyle"; some explore local BDSM clubs; others indulge in the occasional threesome; some have a six-month open, six-month monogamous marriage; while others give their partner the rare hall pass. Polyamorists focus on "maintaining consensual, openly conducted, multiple-partner relationships in which both men and women have negotiated access to additional partners outside of the traditional committed couple," according to polyamory researcher Elisabeth Sheff.

Polyamory isn't cheating, swinging, or polygamy—having more than one spouse at a time, which is illegal in the United States, Sheff notes. Not everyone embracing an alt lifestyle is accepting of the various ways in which that plays out; some poly people can't wrap their heads around swingers because they don't understand why people are in it without any desire to connect emotionally. Swingers, on the other hand, don't understand why polys would want so much emotional entanglement. From their perspective, they're mostly in it for the fun and the sex.

What's the benefit of having an Open Marriage? Besides the obvious—sex with other people (and that, for many people, might be reason enough!)—an Open Marriage offers you a way to truly expand yourself. You can experience different expressions of vulnerability, deepen your connections to others, confront your fears about jealousy and perhaps intimacy, challenge whatever control issues or possessiveness you have, enhance your self-esteem, learn more about your sexuality, and explore fantasies and even bisexuality safely. Some suggest that monogamy's exclusivity and attendant jealousies and sense of ownership over another—sold to society through the rose-colored lens of true love and romance—keeps women emotionally dependent on men and continues to fuel the idea that one man can, and should, fulfill all her needs. Meanwhile, monogamy for men goes counter to their innate need to "'spread genes' by broadcasting sperm." If you've gotten this far into the book, you already know how that's working. It's not.

We're not suggesting that consensual non-monogamy is better than monogamy or that monogamy is better than consensual non-monogamy, and even the studies we looked at don't advocate for one over the other. It's just that people have been brought up to believe that monogamy or mono-normativity is "just the way things are"; the assumption is that committed couples are sexually exclusive and that no one has sex outside the relationship. Judging by how many people are cheating on their partners, however, it's clear that isn't quite true. We believe it's society's unquestioned assumptions that are causing problems.

And infidelity, besides being emotionally painful, can be dangerous to your health; those who indulge in it tend to not practice safe sex, while those in consensual non-monogamy arrangements do. Not only that, but we know that people who have their partner's permission to fool around are more likely to use condoms correctly.

Of course, we are not trying to convince you that you should consider an Open Marriage as a way to avoid getting sexually transmitted diseases. Nor are we trying to convert you to become polyamorous or a swinger, especially since neither of us is in a non-monogamous relationship. We're not hypocrites. We are, however, suggesting that you question and explore what you might prefer—and, just as important, *why* you prefer it—before you commit yourself to another person who may or may not have different ideas about it. Once you're clear about where you stand, you'll be better able to express that openly and honestly with your partner and give him or her a safe and respectful place to do the same. And it's a conversation that needs to be had throughout your relationship; your needs and desires will likely change from your newlywed days to your new-parent days to your empty-nester days.

You may already know that sexual monogamy and lifetime pair-bonding is rare among animals. Well, it's not much different for humans. Sometimes, humans have not only been able to recognize that but also honor it. As sociologist Stephanie Coontz notes:

> In many societies of the past, sexual loyalty was not a high priority. The expectation of mutual fidelity is a rather recent invention. Numerous cultures have allowed husbands to seek sexual gratification outside marriage. Less frequently, but often enough to challenge common preconceptions, wives have also been allowed to do this without threatening the marriage. In a study of 109 societies, anthropologists found that only 48 forbade extramarital sex to both husbands and wives.

Regardless of whether humans are designed to be monogamous or not, part of the beauty and privilege of being human is that people can and often do change what's been biologically—or culturally—programmed so they can evolve and become more authentic.

"One of the most valuable things we can learn from open sexual lifestyles is that our programming is changeable," write Dossie Easton and Catherine A. Liszt in *The Ethical Slut*, considered the bible for open relationships. "Starting by questioning all the ways we have been told our sexuality ought to be, we can begin to edit and rewrite our old tapes. So by breaking the rules, we both free and empower ourselves."

THE UPSIDE OF OPENING UP

Sometimes couples break the rules to adapt to a new life situation. A woman from Australia wrote to us that, when her husband of twenty years became an invalid a decade ago and could no longer perform sexually, he gave her his blessing to take on lovers. She cares for him—emotionally, physically, and financially—and says they have "a loving, caring relationship that is as intimate, pleasant, and comfortable as it can be given his health issues." Still, it hasn't been easy:

> I cannot acknowledge my lover's existence in many contexts because people jump to the conclusion that I am cheating on my sick partner, and I do not have the emotional energy to go around justifying myself and explaining and defending polyamory to everyone all the time. I'm a middle-aged professional—I don't want to be the vanguard for new relationship models and be a target for gossip and hate for my lifestyle. I have already had one major incident at work where I was seen having lunch with a lover and kissing him and had a (male) coworker vehemently denounce me as a "cheating slut" in front of the entire office for it.

For those who don't know and don't understand this woman's plight, it's all too easy to denounce her overtly, as in this case, or covertly by badmouthing her to others. Now you may better understand why so many people who choose to have an Open Marriage tend to be quiet about it.

But there's another kind of non-monogamy for when couples just want to break the rules for a short time. It's called negotiated monogamy. Michelle, whom you met in the chapter on Companionship Marriage, says she's a sexual woman at heart, but, in all her previous relationships, the passion died out after about two or three years. While there were no great sexual sparks between her and her husband, Craig, he had all the qualities to make a great dad and companion. So they wed. "I thought, 'I'm not that passionate with this guy, but I'm way more compatible in many ways. And since it dies out anyway, I'd better be with someone I like.'"

When their second child was about a year old, their comfortable relationship started petering out, and Michelle felt frustrated; not only wasn't she getting the passion she craved, but now she also wasn't even getting the great companionship. She suggested counseling numerous times. He balked. Then she suggested that they have their sexual needs met by others in a don't-ask-don't-tell arrangement. "That really shocked him. And yet it was like that conversation never happened."

They didn't have a formal arrangement or even a loose one, for that matter. But something had to change. Over the summer, Michelle slept with someone. The same week, she saw pop-up ads from AshleyMadison.com and AdultFriendFinder.com on Craig's laptop. "I had about thirty minutes of feeling really rattled by it, and then the next hour was incredible relief," she says.

Except Craig hadn't been looking to hook up; he admitted to looking at porn, which explained the pop-ups (although the pop-ups were sites for affairs, not for porn, which may have been tempting if he were ready to take a big step outside the marriage). She had already confessed to her affair, which led to a period of difficult conversations and soul-searching.

But the experience opened up Michelle's eyes in surprising ways. "I felt like I took responsibility for my own sexuality away from my husband's plate, and I no longer resented him for not meeting that need. And with that resentment gone, I fell crazy back in love with him over the course of the summer while I was still sleeping with this other guy. And I just appreciate about him everything that I'd appreciated about him all along. I thought, this is bizarre. I certainly didn't expect this effect, but I like it."

Now they are negotiating a more formalized arrangement, but they are still unsure how it will work. Craig met someone, and that has helped make their experimentations more equitable. Even though it's sometimes hard and not ideal, at least they're doing something different and that, she believes, is better than what they were before—"strangers raising kids together."

A lot of her female friends are in the same boat. Many are

cheating. And Michelle is not surprised. "We are the first divorce generation to reach middle-age, so we're hitting the age when our parents got divorced and we're looking around seeing a lot of the same dissatisfactions that they experienced. But we're not necessarily willing to just throw out our marriages. We're like, okay, divorce wasn't ideal either, so let's try some other options."

Ironically, Craig has benefitted, she's benefitted, and their marriage has benefitted from their fledgling experimental arrangement. "We both still have the goal of dying in each other's arms. What we're figuring out now is can we have an open marriage and still maintain a bond with each other, and, in many ways in these months, we've been way more real and closer than we ever have in our eighteen years together," she says. "It's the first time he's allowed himself to be emotionally vulnerable and accessible and really truly present, instead of living the life he thinks he's supposed to live or be the guy he's supposed to be. I feel that I'm really seeing him for who he is, and I love that."

WHEN AN ILLICIT AFFAIR ISN'T AN OPTION

Brad and Kira, who got married in their early twenties, have also learned valuable lessons from their foray into non-monogamy. Less than two years into their marriage, Kira felt a strong attraction to a coworker. It wasn't much of a surprise to Brad because Kira had been a virgin when the Pacific Northwest couple met in college.

It was Kira's suggestion that they open up their marriage. Having an affair wasn't an option. She didn't want to hurt Brad—she loved him—and she didn't want to lie to him. She had seen how infidelity damaged her own family growing up. So, she read the writings of philosopher Bertrand Russell, a proponent of open marriage, and found the language to suggest that they bust free from monogamy.

"While it was totally a difficult decision and a difficult time, philosophically he agreed with me . . . I referenced the reading I had done and said, 'You know, people *really* do this,' and I think that helped," Kira says.

What also helped was the fact that they were about to leave the state in a few months for a new career opportunity. They agreed to open things up in the short term and end their sexual explorations when they moved so they could make a fresh start in their new home. That doesn't mean they didn't struggle with jealousy, especially Brad, since it was Kira's idea. She admits they didn't have a strategy to handle that. "We endured it. We talked about it."

After their exploration ended, Kira says she realized how happy she is to be in a monogamous relationship. Juggling schedules took a lot of work, and, a few times, she felt like she was becoming emotionally attached to her lovers, which "seemed kind of dangerous," she admits.

Still, they believe there was something incredibly brave and empowering about their decision; a "badge of courage," is how Kira describes it. They learned that they could make up their own rules and take risks in their relationship, and, frankly, doing something different than the mainstream together—without any deception—was exciting.

"Our sex life was better because we felt invigorated," Brad says. "We found each other very compelling because we were both embarking on this experiment and it takes a certain kind of bravery, and we found that attractive in each other and ourselves."

Kira adds that it "really expanded my world, my sense of myself, and what I am capable of, good and bad. I knew I was capable of hurting him. You think life is going to be one way or that marriage is going to be one way, but you have a lot more choices than you think you do. Somehow that made me feel more empowered and more responsible."

Now that they have a child, Kira's no longer interested in revisiting an open marriage; Brad, however, is. The two are exploring having him go to sex clubs on his own. Kira's discovery that she prefers monogamy is an important one. The only way people can fully commit to a monogamous relationship in a responsible and long-lasting way is by allowing themselves to explore a variety of sexual and intimate relationships first.

I CAN'T COMMIT UNTIL I CAN NOT COMMIT

Bella also was a virgin when she met Ted. They married when she was just twenty, as many women in the South do. Thirty years into their forty-five-year childfree marriage, she experienced a series of family deaths. Then 9/11 happened. The fragility of life startled her, and she began to reflect on the things she missed out on by marrying so young.

An affair was not an option for her either, even though she finds monogamy ridiculous. "I care about him, I don't want to hurt his feelings," she says of Ted. "I also knew he'd divorce me in a second because that's who he is."

They went to a few workshops on threesomes, and one day found themselves in bed with another man. Then they went to a sex club as part of an intimate group of friends and had a few more threesomes, together and separately. For a trip abroad, Bella got a hall pass and spent a glorious night with a much younger man. "It's a great ego boost," the sixty-five-year-old Northern California resident acknowledges.

But Ted never really felt 100 percent comfortable with their experimentations. "He's a one-woman man," Bella sighs. So after a little more than two years of sexual play, they returned to monogamy. Still, their brief journey into an Open Marriage transformed their relationship for the better. "It's actually made us more open to other kinds of nonsexual experiences. We do a lot more social stuff than we used to do," Bella says.

It isn't for everybody, she observes. "I think you have to be very committed to each other and negotiate and communicate whatever differences come up. You have to know how to communicate in a way that you don't hurt your partner's feelings and can respect your partner's point of view. We have very similar upbringings, our basic values are the same or similar, and even we had trouble with that."

She isn't sure it's better or worse than infidelity; she's watched half of her female friends have affairs. An Open Marriage is "a more honest way, but who knows what's better for different people? For some people, that's part of the allure—the secrecy," she observes.

What about jealousy? As the couples above mention, it happens. Of course, it happens to couples in monogamous relationships, too. It's part of people's genetic makeup as well as what we all pick up culturally. It's what you do with that jealousy that matters.

According to research by David M. Buss, author of *The Dangerous Passion: Why Jealousy Is as Necessary as Love and Sex*, nearly all men and women have had at least one extreme bout of jealousy. A third indicated that they sometimes have a hard time controlling their jealousy, and some said that they have felt jealous enough that they wanted to hurt someone (and, indeed, jealousy is the leading cause of spousal murders).

One thing people tend to do is not admit their jealous feelings— to themselves or their partners. If you did, however, you would be able to explore what's behind your jealousy—are you afraid you'll lose your partner, are you feeling shut out, does it make you feel inadequate?

"Jealousy forces you to consider one of the great conundrums that every person faces: how to want another person madly and at the same time grant her her freedom as a person with her own life and fate," writes psychotherapist and author Thomas Moore. "All the questions with which you torture yourself, all your doubts, all your shifting back and forth—all of these tools of jealousy twist you out of your immaturity and eventually teach you how to love."

And, that love includes compersion, a word coined by the poly community to express the joy you feel for your partner as he or she discovers love outside your relationship. It's similar to the joy you feel when something good happens to someone close, like a good friend or a favorite relative, and most people are capable of that. Is it easy? No. Still, it's exciting to know that there are alternatives to feeling jealousy in relationships.

WHAT ABOUT THE KIDS?

You're ready to have an Open Marriage. You and your spouse have read a few books, attended a few workshops, engaged in some online forums, and spent countless hours setting up the parameters of this exciting—and scary—new marital model. There's only one piece that seems to be troubling—what about the kids?

In truth, there isn't a lot of information available on how open marriages impact children. Perhaps no one has done more research on it than sociologist Elisabeth Sheff. After following poly families for fifteen years (her focus was on families with three or more adults in committed relationships and who shared childrearing), she published the results in her late-2013 book *The Polyamorists Next Door: Inside Multiple-Partner Relationships and Families.*

While she says poly kids can be as "obnoxious, defiant, and irritating" as anyone else's kids, they appear to be doing pretty well. Many seem to benefit from the multiple adults who come into their life and dote on them and often act as role models—confirming that childrearing really does "take a village" (which appears to support anthropologist Sarah Blaffer Hrdy's idea of shared caregiving, or alloparenting). Still, some kids experience pain and loss when a breakup means a partner they've come to love leaves the family.

Most are well aware of the stigma of their parents' lifestyle, but just like children of LGBT parents, they learn how to deal with it. Because polyamorists generally don't talk openly about their out-of-the-box families and prefer to stay under the radar, poly kids are easily able to blend in as "normals." Or, they pass themselves off as children of divorce—since so many kids have multiple parents and stepsiblings from multiple marriages nowadays, it's pretty easy to appear like any other child of divorce. But being outed and labeled the "weird kid" would be pretty devastating for them.

The problem with getting a good handle on what life is really like for kids growing up in non-monogamous families is that poly people are often hesitant to talk to researchers because of negative stereotypes that poly families are at higher risk for sexual abuse or out of fear that they might lose custody of their children.

Of course, not every open family is a poly family, as *Polyamory in the 21st Century* author Deborah Anapol observes; many more children are being raised in open marriages, and the true impacts of how that will shape their experiences "have not even begun to be considered, except by theorists and the parents themselves, let alone researched." From Anapol's own experience, poly kids don't typically become poly adults. In fact, they tend to embrace serial monogamy. "As I often joke," she writes, "if you want your children to be monogamous, practice polyamory!"

NON-MONOGAMY CALLS FOR CONFIDENCE AND TRUST

For whom does consensual non-monogamy work? Kira says it's important to have confidence in yourself, believe in what you're doing, and know your boundaries. Being outgoing helps.

"For a lot of people, it doesn't even occur to them that they can be anything other than monogamous, and they get into a situation and then realize they maybe feel differently. I also feel monogamy can be dangerous even without sleeping with other people. Just having a sense of your own sexuality, being attracted to other people, being able to flirt with other people; when you can't do that, it just shuts down a part of you. It changes who you are in your marriage and so long-term, that can be really damaging," she told us.

For Bryce, trust is key. "A lot of people don't trust their partner enough, and people don't want to share. I'd recommend that you are a couple that has a super amount of trust and don't have a lot of jealousy issues."

For Dana, it's about the confidence you have in yourself and in your partner. "It boils down to what type of human being is each person in this relationship. Human beings want to have sexual relations with more than one partner for the rest of their life. They may want to be with that one person, and be soul mates and connect with love, they may not want to have an actual relationship with somebody else, but I think sex is sex. It's primal. Married, happily or not, they want to have sex with somebody else."

While you may not feel the same way, that sex is just sex, Dana is right—who are the people who are committing to a marriage? What are their morals? Are they honest and open, trusting and trustworthy, committed to being the best person they can be and supportive of their partner's desire to do the same? We hope you wouldn't marry anyone less than that. And if you have that and are that, you, too, are free to create *your* marriage.

WHAT'S GOOD ABOUT AN OPEN MARRIAGE

- You get to have sex with other people while maintaining an intimate relationship.

- You get to have deeper connections to and experience vulnerability with others.

- You may have a deeper understanding and appreciation of your partner.

- If you and your partner have different sexual drives, you can each feel satisfied.

- It allows you to safely express your sexuality.

- It may fulfill your exhibitionist or voyeuristic sides.

- You can explore the many ways in which humans are capable of loving others at the same time.

- You may feel good knowing that you are truly giving your partner what he or she wants, and your partner is doing the same for you.

- More and different partners allow you to experience yourself in different ways.

- It may make your marriage more passionate.

- Working with jealousy may lead to a better understanding of unconditional love.

- You may become more committed to being monogamous.

- It gives you a safe way to explore bisexuality.

- It gives you an opportunity to explore fantasies.

- It may increase your self-esteem.

- It may be a boost to your partner's and your sex life.

- You may feel pleasure in being a sexual outlier.

WHAT'S NOT SO GOOD ABOUT AN OPEN MARRIAGE

- You may feel jealousy.
- You may be subject to misunderstanding and judgment from others.
- You may experience shame or sin.
- You may experience fear of losing your partner to someone else.
- It may be stressful.
- You may feel insecure.
- You may still experience infidelity.
- It may tear apart the marriage if you and your partner don't have a solid relationship.
- It may take more time management and coordination than you can handle.
- It may prevent you from creating a healthy attachment to your partner.
- You may become emotionally attached to someone else.
- Your partner may become emotionally attached to someone else.
- Your partner may leave you for someone else.
- Your experience, positive and negative, may depend on your gender.
- You may feel cognitive dissonance (when your beliefs don't match up with your reality) if you're not truly committed to the idea.
- You may feel that you settled.
- It may not live up to your expectations.
- If you're a parent, you may have concerns about how your choices may impact your children.
- You may feel guilty for wanting more.
- You may feel that you were talked into it.

HOW TO MAKE AN OPEN MARRIAGE WORK

Whether you're starting off in an Open Marriage or restructuring an existing marriage, you'll need to communicate well and keep talking about it. You and your partner need to agree to the terms of your arrangement; there are a lot of good books and websites you can turn to for advice as well as professional help. Written agreements are best to minimize the chance of a misunderstanding, and you'll want to make sure that you agree on what to do if one of you becomes uncomfortable with the arrangement. The idea of an Open Marriage is to enhance your relationship; if you have any hidden agendas (like easing your exit from your marriage), it's not a good idea.

This marriage may be right for you if:

- You are okay with ignoring or gently responding to how others perceive your marriage.
- It doesn't bother you if others judge you.
- You have a healthy sense of self.
- You're a good communicator.
- You are open-minded.
- You trust yourself and your partner.
- You value honesty.
- You are comfortable taking risks.
- You identify with being a nonconformist.
- You enjoy creativity within relationships.
- You are able to let go of negative beliefs that you don't deserve to be nurtured and loved.
- You are able to make strong, intimate connections with others.
- You have no hidden agendas.
- You wish to expand your relationship and yourself.
- You have support from your partner, and you are able to support him or her.
- You understand jealousy is something you can choose or choose not to harbor.
- Passion, freedom, and self-expression are more important to you than physical exclusivity.

- You are respectful to your various partners and yourself.
- You are able to let go of possessiveness.
- You are good at multitasking.
- You thrive on intensity.
- You enjoy variety.
- You have an appreciation for others' differences and unique qualities.
- You are a good problem-solver.
- You value autonomy.
- You have a good grasp of and respect for boundaries.
- You're flexible.
- You have good emotional intelligence.
- You hold yourself accountable.
- You respect the importance of safe sex.
- You believe that you are responsible for getting your own needs met.
- You take responsibility for your own emotions.
- You are self-reliant.
- You are curious.
- You are good at self-reflection.
- You are not afraid to experience the depth of your feelings.
- You have a good moral compass.

IS AN OPEN MARRIAGE RIGHT FOR ME?

If you're wondering whether or not you're cut out for an Open Marriage, here are a few questions you might want to ask yourself (some may not be applicable if you are already married and are seeking to renegotiate your marriage):

- What are my reasons for marrying?
- What attracts me about an Open Marriage?

- What do I fear about an Open Marriage?

- In what ways would an Open Marriage make my life better?

- In what ways would an Open Marriage make my life worse?

- How important is sexual fidelity to me?

- Why have I been monogamous?

- In what way has monogamy been easy for me?

- In what way has monogamy been hard for me?

- Have I ever been non-monogamous? Why or why not?

- In what ways do I believe sex is just sex?

- In what ways do I believe sex is an expression of love?

- How do I know if I can love more than one person at a time?

- How do I know if I can have sex with someone without loving him or her?

- How do I know if I can love your partner and still have sex with someone else?

- Why do I believe you can trust myself?

- When have I not been able to trust myself?

- How easy is it for me to trust other people?

- What makes me feel jealous?

- When have I been jealous in a romantic relationship?

- What did I do with that jealousy?

- In what ways do I get emotionally attached to others?

- When am I most confident?

- What makes me feel insecure in relationships?

- How have I overcome insecurity in relationships?

- In what ways am I possessive?

- How have I addressed that possessiveness?

- In what ways has my religious upbringing or family-of-origin messages impacted my sex life positively and negatively?

- How have I addressed my attractions to others with your partner?
- How have I addressed my partner's attractions to others?

READ MORE

. . . .

Curious about how to make this marital model work? Here are some books to read for insight and guidance:

- *Against Love: A Polemic* by Laura Kipnis (Vintage, 2004).
- *The Dangerous Passion: Why Jealousy Is as Necessary as Love and Sex* by David M. Buss (Free Press, 2000).
- *The Ethical Slut: A Practical Guide to Polyamory, Open Relationships, and Other Adventures* by Dossie Easton and Janet W. Hardy (Celestial Arts, 2009).
- *The Future of Love: The Power of the Soul in Intimate Relationships* by Daphne Rose Kigma (Main Street Books, 1999).
- *The New Monogamy: Redefining Your Relationship After Infidelity* by Tammy Nelson, PhD (New Harbinger Publications, 2013).
- *What Do Women Want? Adventures in the Science of Female Desire* by Daniel Bergner (Ecco, 2013).
- *Open: Love, Sex, and Life in an Open Marriage* by Jenny Block (Seal Press, 2009).
- *Open Marriage: A New Life Style for Couples* by George O'Neill and Nena O'Neill (M. Evans & Company, 1984).
- *Opening Up: A Guide to Creating and Sustaining Open Relationships* by Tristan Taormino (Cleis Press, 2009).
- *Polyamory in the 21st Century* by Deborah Anapol (Rowman & Littlefield Publishers, 2012).
- *Understanding Non-Monogamies* by Dr. Meg Barker and Darren Langdridge (Routledge, 2009).
- *Redefining Our Relationships: Guidelines for Responsible Open Relationships* by Wendy-O-Matik (Defiant Times Press, 2002).

- *Sex at Dawn: The Prehistoric Origins of Modern Sexuality* by Christopher Ryan and Cacilda Jethá (Harper, 2002).

OPEN MARRIAGE TAKEAWAYS

- An Open Marriage is ideal for two people who are not monogamists but who like the idea of being married.

- A higher value is placed on marital stability than marital monogamy.

- An Open Marriage allows long-term marrieds to enjoy the excitement of being sexual with new people.

- An Open Marriage agreement is much more respectful than having an illicit affair.

- A spouse's sexual needs do not all have to be met by one person.

- An Open Marriage couple enjoys a deep, trusting relationship filled with intimacy and shared sexual experiences.

- An Open Marriage takes away the element of deceit that can often be more devastating to the one cheated on than the sex act itself.

- Those who practice consensual non-monogamy practice safe sex more than those who have affairs on their spouse.

- An Open Marriage acknowledges that humans are sexual beings who may have physical attractions to a number of people at the same time.

- Being open with your partner about your sexual needs can create a deeper emotional connection with him or her.

Chapter 10

TO PRE OR NOT TO PRE WHEN YOUR MATE POPS THE QUESTION

"Marriage is not just a private love story but also a social and economical contract of the strictest order. If it weren't, there wouldn't be thousands of municipal, state, and federal laws pertaining to our matrimonial union."
—Elizabeth Gilbert

*E*ven people who appreciate horror novels and movies might be frightened out of their wits if their spouse-to-be announced, "Honey, I'd like you to sign a prenup."

A prenuptial agreement (or prenup) is a legal agreement a couple enters into before they get married. There are a lot of misconceptions about prenups, and, because of that, far too many people are afraid of or reject the notion of prenups. As with many aspects of traditional marriage, that thinking is antiquated and small-minded. As you have seen earlier in the book, marriage is a legal contract. To ignore that reality and enter into that legal contract before discussing "business" is not only impractical but also foolish, regardless of what kind of marriage you have.

The marital models in this book require you to take off your rose-colored glasses and romantic notions about love and see marriage as a wonderful union with goals, responsibilities, and ways to measure how well you are doing, as a couple and as a spouse. You can't determine if something is successful or not unless you are extremely clear about the tasks at hand. Writing it down and mutually agreeing on what you're doing will help you hold yourself and each other accountable. You have a different objective than just "lifelong" love and "happily-ever-after"—it isn't about building *a* life with someone, it's about building *a specific kind of life*.

It's no coincidence that 20 percent of marriages in which one spouse has been married before seeks a prenup, compared with just 5 percent of first-time marriers. All it takes is a divorce to get people to understand that marriage is still very much about money and property. Those who have previously wed and, in one form or another, got burned, likely want to avoid making the same mistake. The spouse who was obliged to pay a lot of money to the former spouse would not want to leave that to chance again, while the spouse who came away empty-handed or felt the outcome of his or her first divorce was unfair wouldn't want to be that naive or vulnerable again.

Most legal and financial experts advise couples to protect themselves. And thankfully, more people are listening, not just the rich and famous who have millions at stake, according to the American Academy of Matrimonial Lawyers, which pays attention to such things. We take the increased interest in prenups as a sign that spouses-to-be are getting smarter and are acknowledging that business and romance can indeed go hand in hand.

We outline below some ideas of what you might want to include in a prenup or, if you are transforming an existing marriage, a postnup—a contract you create after you are already married—for each of the models in the book. But, just for fun, let's test your knowledge about prenups first and then do some myth-busting. And maybe, after that, you'll see that your misconceived notions have been holding you back from thinking a prenup is for you.

WHAT DO YOU KNOW ABOUT PRENUPS?

True or False:

1. A prenup is only for the wealthy. ....T or F

2. A prenup only protects one of the spouses. ....T or F

3. If you're both broke, you don't need a prenup ....T or F

4. You don't need a lawyer to write your prenup.
   You can write it yourselves...T or F

5. Only people who don't trust each other need prenups...........T or F

6. You can address fidelity in your prenup..................................T or F

7. It's easier to come up with agreements when you're on
   good terms than when you're on bad terms............................T or F

8. You can outline your financial goals in a prenup ....T or F

9. A prenup has to be in writing to be enforceable....................T or F

10. A postnup (like a prenup but executed after
    you're already married) carries more weight
    than a prenup ....T or F

11. Once your prenup is signed, it can't be changed.................T or F

12. You can decide who gets the family dog in a prenup ....T or F

13. You can make decisions about child
    custody in a prenup ....T or F

14. You can decide how many children you want
    to have (if any) in a prenup ....T or F

15. Prenups can set agreements for the marriage,
    not just for a potential breakup (for example,
    both spouses will be expected to maintain
    employment during the entire length of the marriage)......T or F

16. A prenup trumps state law..T or F

17. Prenups work best when you're older ....T or F

18. You should hire your own attorney to
    advise you on the prenup ....T or F

19. It's okay to ask your betrothed to sign a
    prenup any time prior to the wedding ....T or F

20. Prenups can be used to clarify and
    memorialize your intentions around
    childbirth and fertility treatment...T or F

NOW LET'S TAKE A LOOK AT THE ANSWERS:

1. A prenup is only for the wealthy. FALSE. But one of the most
   frequently preconceived notions about prenups is that they are
   only for rich people who want to protect their assets. The truth
   is, most people can benefit from outlining who will get what in
   the event of a breakup.

2. A prenup only protects one of the spouses. FALSE. Prenups
   can—and often do—protect both spouses. As long as you both
   have input, you can make sure both of you are protected.

3. If you're both broke, you don't need a prenup. FALSE. If you
   have no assets to protect, you may not feel it's worth getting a
   prenup. However, you can still opt to get one to outline what
   your expectations are around your future goals and prospective
   financial well-being, as well as to discuss how any debt you
   accrue will be handled. (For example, student loan debt that
   a spouse comes into the marriage with may be paid off by the
   couple or not.)

4. You don't need a lawyer to write your prenup. You can write it
   yourselves. IT DEPENDS. Check your state laws. Most attorneys
   will tell you that you need to have it properly drawn up and
   signed off on by an attorney. Even Nolo, a leading publisher
   of do-it-yourself legal books and software to help laypeople
   represent themselves legally where possible, advises that while
   you can certainly do your own research, it's best to get legal
   representation for prenups.

5. Only people who don't trust each other need prenups.
FALSE. Getting a prenup actually says you understand the
fragility of life and that you are not in denial that anything is
possible—even your worst-case scenario. There are just way
too many factors that come into play in life. Yes, it is divorce-
preparedness, which is why many people don't like the idea of
them, believing that if you talk about divorce before you even
marry, you are setting yourself up for divorce. Except that is
wrong. Prenups establish agreements so you know you're both
playing by the same rules. Far from impeding trust, making
agreements fosters trust.

6. You can address fidelity in your prenup. TRUE. There is a
"fidelity clause" that you can write into your prenup. If you
trust your partner, you probably cannot imagine that he or
she would cheat on you. As much as we hate to be the bearer
of bad news, it happens—more than you'd care to think (as we
detailed in previous chapters). Fidelity clauses are not valid in
every state, so be sure to check with your attorney to know if
it's an option for you.

7. It's easier to come up with agreements when you're on good
terms than when you're on bad terms. TRUE. Well, of course.

8. You can outline your financial goals in a prenup. TRUE. Prenups
are not just to help you plan for life after your marriage ends;
they can be used to map out financial goals, child and parenting
goals, business venture goals, and much more. It's your "financial
mission statement."

9. A prenup has to be in writing to be enforceable. TRUE. The
Statue of Frauds requires that a prenup must be in writing to
be enforceable.

10. A postnup carries more weight than a prenup. TRUE. Once
you are married, each spouse has a fiduciary duty to the other.
Each spouse must make full disclosure of all material facts
and information to the best of his or her knowledge regarding

the existence, characterization, and valuation of community assets and debts. Each spouse must also act with all of the following: the highest standard of care and the highest order of good faith and fair dealing, among other things. Although your spouse-to-be undoubtedly expects you to be honest, this standard does not legally apply before you are married. Unfortunately, a fair number of future-spouses hide or diminish the value of their assets.

11. Once your prenup is signed, it can't be changed. FALSE. Prenups may be changed, but, as you learned from question 10, if you renegotiate the terms of the contract post-wedding date, it's no longer a prenup but a postnup.

12. You can decide who gets the family dog in a prenup. TRUE. You can absolutely delineate who gets Fifi or Fido. In fact, this is often one of the greatest points of contention with couples, as many more couples are sharing custody of pets these days.

13. You can make decisions about child custody in a prenup. FALSE. It would be nearly impossible to predict ahead of time all the factors that determine the best custody arrangements for children, and it's against public policy to do so. Even if you were to stipulate certain conditions in the premarital agreement, they would likely get thrown out of court by the judge.

14. You can decide how many children you want to have (if any) in a prenup. TRUE. You can certainly state how many children you'd like to have in your prenup as an ideal, but what is enforceable will depend on your state's laws. However, this is a complex question that requires legal counsel.

15. Prenups can set agreements for the marriage, not just for a potential breakup (for example, both spouses will be expected to maintain employment during the entire length of the marriage). TRUE. As you'll learn later in this chapter, many aspects of marriage can be spelled out.

16. A prenup trumps state law. FALSE. Prenups merely allow you to opt out of state law on some issues.

17. Prenups work best when you're older. MOSTLY TRUE. Prenups generally work as well as they are written and as well as they hold up in court, no matter how old or young the signers are. That said, despite the new generation of young billionaires like Facebook founder Mark Zuckerberg (no word on whether he had a prenup when he wed in 2012, but we'd be willing to bet that he did), older people tend to have more wealth, and prenups are designed to protect assets. And since many older people are more likely to have a prior marriage, which may have ended in an ugly, messy divorce, they are more likely to want a prenup if they marry again.

18. You should hire your own attorney to advise you on the prenup. TRUE. In fact, some states require you to hire your own attorney. If you don't have proper representation, there's a risk that the entire agreement will be invalidated. Keep in mind that the cliché "you get what your pay for" is true in this case.

19. It's okay to ask your betrothed to sign a prenup any time prior to the wedding. IT DEPENDS. This is a trick question, but it's an important one for which you must know the answer. Check with your attorney and your state laws. Asking someone to sign a prenup with no discussion and no legal representation thirty minutes prior to the ceremony—when your loved ones are gathered and you are a vision of white (or black-and-white)—is *not* a great idea. Presenting a prenup under these circumstances will likely invalidate it, provided your spouse can prove this was how it was executed.

20. Prenups can be used to clarify and memorialize your intentions around childbirth and fertility treatment. TRUE. Despite the fact that this clause may not hold up in court, the value in writing about your intentions to freeze an embryo or undertake IVF is that it shows the court what your intentions were at the time of marriage.

PRENUPS FOR YOUR PARTICULAR FLAVOR OF MARRIAGE

Now that you have a better understanding of prenups and postnups, let's explore what prenups might want to address for each of the marital models in this book. But first, a warning: we are not lawyers, so what is presented below is no substitute for sound legal advice. Our intention is solely to give you a few ideas of what you may want to consider when you, your future spouse, and your attorneys are ready to craft your agreement. In all cases, we recommend that you defer to the judgment of the professional you hired who knows the local laws as well as your situation intimately.

STARTER MARRIAGE

In many ways, this is the perfect time to do a prenup because you have a blank slate, meaning that you don't have kids or debts and responsibilities from a previous marriage. You and your partner can create any number of agreements and goals for your time-limited future together.

Of course, the Starter Marriage prenup is also a little tricky because, under public policy, you can't encourage divorce. So rather than it being referred to as a prenup, your time-limited contract is best referred to as a term agreement. In this agreement, you can outline how you would like the next five years (or two or ten, depending on the agreed-upon term) to look and what you'd like to accomplish. The number one rule of this marriage, however, is that you both must agree not to have children. You must put that in writing, as well as the mutually agreed-to birth control methods you will use and what you plan to do in the event of a pregnancy. Depending on your age, you might also want to include a provision for paying for freezing your eggs—is he responsible for paying a share even though she may go on to use her eggs with some other partner in the event they don't stay together?—and establish who "owns" the eggs.

Another important aspect to the agreement might include the division of labor. It seems silly to have to put that in writing, but if you and your partner agree that having an egalitarian marriage is important to you, it is imperative to spell out who does what so there are no false assumptions and expectations. Since many couples fight over chores, and since many women tend to do more of them, having something in writing will keep you accountable to each other.

Another thing newlyweds have problems with is communication. While you can't make your partner be a better communicator, you can set the ground rules of what your communication will look like. Think you need to take some nonviolent communication classes together? Write it down. Do you want to have a weekly or a monthly or a yearly check-in to see where you both are in your goals? Write it down. You certainly will want to agree to when you should start talking about renewing your contract, or not, as the deadline nears. And, you will want to include a stipulation that each of you be honest about how things are going well in advance of the deadline; if what you have been hearing from your partner all along is that things are great and then, right before it's time to renew, boom—she tells you that she's been miserable, that would indicate that there has been some level of deception. Remember, the purpose of this marriage is to gain self-knowledge and an understanding of what marriage feels like and how you act in it. If you are not being honest with each other, you will have learned nothing.

Another essential is agreeing to finances. Since many people are marrying later and come into a partnership with nest eggs of their own and perhaps even property, these will need to be addressed. So will any student loan debt. While you're at it, you or your partner may want to go to grad school; you'll need to figure out how that will impact finances, household chores, and whether you will have to move to another city, state, or country, perhaps requiring one of you to give up a job.

The rest of the contract is really up to you and your spouse to design. If you want to add a fidelity agreement (or if you are incorporating all or some of the elements of an Open Marriage), spell it out. It's also a good idea to discuss whether you will commit to therapy if problems arise. Aspirations such as wanting to save a chunk of money by the end of the term may be included. If vows are renewed, you would be able to put that money toward a baby fund or the purchase of a home; if you split up, it could come in handy to pay for legal fees to process your dissolution.

COMPANIONSHIP MARRIAGE

You may be younger, you may be older, but you don't plan to have children together as you enter into a Companionship Marriage (although one or both of you may have children from a previous marriage,). You're also not marrying for money. You may be in a similar place financially as your spouse, or you may not be. The bottom line is that you are partnering with someone whose company you enjoy and with whom you hope to spend many years being friends.

As you read in the chapter, this is often the marriage of childfree couples. But if you have older children from a previous relationship, you might want to detail whether they can stay in your house when they visit and if you will help them out financially, say to purchase a house. Blending households, even when the children are adults, adds many layers of complications—it's good to be clear about your expectations. It's also important to know that, without a prenup, state law would dictate who would get what—property, money, and other assets. In some cases, a spouse might not be entitled to keep the house she is living in if her spouse dies without a will. Instead, it might go to his children. That could be devastating—especially if there is some bad blood. Write it down.

As with every other marital model, you will want to address domestic roles, especially if you are marrying for the first time and are used to having your house and stuff look a certain way, or if you raised your family in a previous marriage and now are not too keen on taking up the role of domestic goddess again. If you can afford it, an agreement on hiring a housekeeper, a gardener, or both might help. A plan for long-term caregiving should be addressed as well.

Another consideration would be what happens if one of you is ready to retire and the other is not. The new retiree may look forward to travel and adventure, which may not be feasible for the still-employed spouse. An agreement of how to balance travel together with solo travel or travel with friends might be helpful.

As with every other model, a couple may choose to renegotiate their Companionship Marriage to transform it into another model or incorporate elements of another model.

PARENTING MARRIAGE

A prenup for a Parenting Marriage will likely be the most elaborate prenup of all the marital models (although an Open Marriage may come close). As divorced parents know, they have to spell out just about everything that pertains to their kids. You will need to do that, too. Yes, it's exhausting.

While this model requires a long list of agreements, two are key—the length of time you and your partner commit to being together (as this is a time-limited contract), and an action plan addressing parenting philosophies. Ideally, parents should commit to stick together for about eighteen years, or the time that their child graduates from high school and is ready for college, a trade school, or employment. The contract will have to extend for each child, as you will want to give your youngest the same stability his or her older siblings have. All of which means you may be married for a long time. While on the surface it will look no different than traditional marriages, which often end at around the same time, when a child graduates high school, it is not, because of all the extensive planning that goes into it and because parents did not come together for love—just to have kids.

That brings up the second key requirement: co-parents must agree on parenting philosophies and styles and have a plan in place to respectfully address how to handle any future schisms. Part of the beauty and perhaps the challenge of this model is that it is structured to be a lot less conflict-ridden than a couple that comes together because of love. This marriage is grounded in expectations that are realistic and in goals that are narrowly focused—to provide a loving, respectful, nourishing, safe, secure, and stable home for children. Therefore, every item you and your partner agree to must have that goal in mind. You may want to seek professional help first, as Rami Aizic and his co-parent did (his story is in the Parenting Marriage chapter), on a one-time or continuing basis, or take parenting classes together; these, too, should be spelled out in your prenup.

Other things to be planned are whether you will live in the same house with your co-parent; how you will financially support your kids; whether one or both of you will be expected to have paid work, and how to accommodate changes in employment such as a job loss, flex time, moving for a new job opportunity, and long-distant commuting; how many children you hope to have and their spacing; if infertility is an issue, deciding if you would adopt or use IVF or both, and how many series you are willing and able to fund; whether you will freeze any eggs or embryos; who will care for the kids— an at-home parent, daycare, nannies, a live-in au pair, or relatives; which schooling options you will choose, such as private, public, homeschooling, and special ed; whether you will vaccinate or not; how to spend leisure and family time; whether you'd like the kids to participate in religious training; and how to save for college. Obviously, inheritance and life insurance are vital topics, as well as guardianship in the event that both you and your spouse die prematurely (these are estate-planning issues).

Because couples typically argue the most about household chores and time caring for the kids—and we don't mean time *playing* with the kids—you and your partner will have to exhaustively detail what your expectations are. Again, one of the goals of this marriage is to reduce household conflict.

Because your children's needs change as they get older, so, too, will your agreement need to change. You should agree to a regular schedule of check-ins, ideally no less than once a year, to anticipate what might need to be adjusted.

And, while the marriage is designed to be renewed (or not) after the agreed-to time is over, things happen. So, you need to have a plan of action in place in the event of a split. Here, too, it is against public policy to encourage divorce in a prenup, so planning as if you are sure your marriage will end isn't appropriate. Planning "in the event of divorce" is fine so you can address the possibility that the marriage will end. If you and your partner stay together, you will need to renegotiate your Parenting Marriage to transform it into another model.

LIVING ALONE TOGETHER (LAT) MARRIAGE

By the nature of this arrangement, addressing the obvious—how long you and your partner will live apart and how often you will see each other—is where you would want to start your prenup. From there, you will need to outline who comes to whom (do you take turns, is there a primary residence, do you meet halfway, etc.); how expenses will be handled (are travel costs shared; are rent, maintenance, and utilities shared, etc.); and how you will stay connected (emails, texts, Skype, etc.) and how often.

If you have children at home, your agreement must include their concerns as well as your spouse's. You might want to make provisions to help avoid the "super-parent" syndrome by hiring help. You and your spouse should also be clear on how frequently you will come home, scheduled family time, how you will keep connected to your children, and allowances for ongoing family counseling to help everyone have a safe place to address their concerns.

If you don't have an Open Marriage as well, a fidelity clause defining what constitutes infidelity in your marriage should be agreed to. You may also want to clarify how much information you need from each other (do you need to know who your spouse is spending time with, what he or she does with off-work time, etc.). You may also want to agree that you should meet each other's coworkers, friends, and neighbors to feel more connected to your partner's other life.

Finally, a plan of action should be agreed to that details what would happen if one spouse lost employment (would you move in together, continue to pay for both places, create a budget for such emergencies?) and what will happen if you agree that you no longer wish to live apart.

As with every other model, a couple may choose to renegotiate their LAT Marriage to transform it into another model or incorporate elements of another model.

COVENANT MARRIAGE

Despite the fact that this marriage is slated to last "for life," Covenant marriers can still have a meaningful prenup. While the premarital agreement can certainly outline what would happen in the event of a dissolution of the marriage (such as, the person who breaks the covenant is not entitled to any of the assets accumulated during the marriage, or will be asked to leave the community or church), this contract may focus more on how the marriage will be set up, including such typical issues as employment, children, religious practice, and financial concerns.

Although most couples that choose this type of marriage tend to be traditionally oriented, that does not necessarily mean you can't create a more egalitarian model, especially in the typical gendered sphere of household chores and childcare. It is clear from the laws in each of the three states that recognize Covenant Marriages that there should be no addiction, abuse, criminal involvement, or abandonment, as those behaviors constitute legitimate grounds for divorce, but this can certainly be included in the prenup as extra "insurance." Given that counseling is an imperative in the Covenant Marriage if problems arise in the marriage, it might be helpful to set an expectation of how soon, how long, and under what circumstances you would seek professional guidance.

SAFETY MARRIAGE

Since this marriage is all about the business of marriage and a prenup is all about the business of marriage, this prenup may read like a corporate partnership compared with the other prenups.

Job descriptions and responsibilities may be laid out: one spouse might be the sole breadwinner, while the other will be in charge of maintaining the household, taking care of the kids, calendaring social events, and perhaps even helping with aspects of a family business. Assets and interests on both sides of that family business, intellectual property or other sources of income, spending allowances, and what goods and services are to be exchanged may all be addressed in this prenup.

There should be a plan of action to address any disruption to the power balance in the couple, such as if the breadwinning spouse loses a job, takes a lower-paying job, returns to school to earn a higher degree, suffers financial devastation, or becomes ill or disabled and unable to work. There should also be provisions if the lesser-earning spouse becomes an equal or higher earner.

Understanding and agreeing about how children will be cared for financially and otherwise will be important. If there are children from other marriages and outgoing spousal support to a former spouse or spouses, that will also need to be factored in.

If the main reason for choosing a Safety Marriage is about financial well-being, an agreement should be made about any expectation of being taken care of if the marriage doesn't last—especially by the one receiving monetary support who may have given up a career in service of the marriage or parenthood.

Paragraphs dealing with fidelity, inheritance, right of survivorship, and the waiving of rights to certain assets are pertinent concerns in a Safety Marriage prenup. And, of course, we think it's important to have a clause that includes if and when the couple would seek professional help if problems arose in the marriage that were too big for them to handle alone.

As with every other model, a couple may choose to renegotiate their Safety Marriage to transform it into another model or incorporate elements of another model.

OPEN MARRIAGE

A relationship with one person is complicated. Having relationships, whether sexual or sexual and emotional, with other people has the potential to be extremely complicated. That's why this prenup will need to clearly spell out the terms of how open sexual relations will be handled by both parties within the marriage and outside it. Because consensual non-monogamy comes in so many varieties, it is impossible to include the many details you and your partner will need to agree to. There are books written on that alone (and that is why many people believe as imperfect as monogamy may be, it's a lot less complicated).

But here are a few basic things you might want to start off with. You and your partner will need to decide the type of sexual exploration you desire—together, apart, or a combination of both. You will need to agree on whether you are poly, are into swinging, enjoy three- and foursomes together, or are willing to give each other the occasional hall pass. And you will need to agree on whether this is your lifestyle or a limited experimentation.

Creating a prenup for a poly family is too much for us to address here, so we are mostly focusing on couples that see themselves as monogamish and are looking for sexual pleasure more than deep, ongoing emotional connections to another person or persons.

The most urgent needs of an Open Marriage prenup address honesty, communication, trust, transparency, time management, safety, and jealousy. You will need to give more thought to establishing the rules governing honesty than anything else. You need to agree if you have a don't-ask-don't-tell arrangement or whether you both want to know all the dirty details. You will also need to agree on how much time you each may spend with others without compromising your partnership.

Other agreements might include discretion in partner choices; same-sex or strictly opposite sex; safe-sex; pregnancy-preventative contraceptives; whether the family home is off limits; in what ways you may change the agreement if and when you have children; and what to do if someone changes his or her mind and wants to close up the marriage. A hugely important consideration is what you will do if a nonmarital partner gets pregnant or if you or your wife gets pregnant by a lover. How will that be handled emotionally and financially?

You get the idea. There are lots of little nooks and crannies where complications and disagreements can occur, so the more you cover, the better. Mutual understanding and agreement of the terms are a must in this marriage.

You may certainly detail all the usual agreements relating to home and work life, spousal and parental duties, and financial issues, but, if you do, you might never get around to the actual sex!

As with every other model, a couple may choose to renegotiate their Open Marriage, to transform it into another model, or incorporate elements of another model into this one.

YOU'RE ON YOUR WAY

As far as fear of prenups goes, we'd like to see that become a thing of the past. Not only do premarital agreements clarify your reasons for marrying, but, as you now know, they also help you set goals for your marriage. It's one thing to make goals; it's another thing to write them down. We can't emphasize enough the importance of writing down your goals.

Words on paper are not vague notions of dreams, aspirations, and hopes. They are a guide, a road map, that holds you accountable, that allows you to measure progress, and that can help keep you on track to continually making the right decisions to help you achieve your heart's desires.

And they can, and should, be frequently discussed and renewed as your life situations change.

READ MORE

Curious about prenups and postnups? Here are some books to read for insight and guidance:

- *1001 Questions to Ask Before You Get Married* by Monica Leahy (McGraw-Hill, 2004).

- *Divorce: Think Financially, Not Emotionally: What Women Need to Know About Securing Their Financial Future Before, During, and After Divorce* by Jeff Landers (Sourced Media Books, 2012).

- *The Hard Questions: 100 Questions to Ask Before You Say "I Do"* by Susan Piver (Tarcher/Putnam, 2007).

- *I Do, You Do ... but Just Sign Here: A Quick and Easy Guide to Cohabitation, Prenuptial and Postnuptial Agreements* by Scott N. Weston and Robert Nachshin (Execuprov Pr, 2004).

- *Prenuptial Agreements: How to Write a Fair and Lasting Contract* by Katherine Stoner and Shae Irving, JD (Nolo Press, 2012).

- *Prenups for Lovers: A Romantic Guide to Prenuptial Agreements* by Arlene Dubin (Random House, 2001).

- *What to Do Before You Say "I Do"* by Susan Ziggy (AuthorHouse, 2013).

Chapter 11

OPEN MIND, OPEN DIALOG

"If you want to do something differently,
you're automatically swimming upstream."
—Judith Stacey, author of *Unhitched: Love, Marriage, and
Family Values from West Hollywood to Western China*

When the sixteenth century astronomer and mathematician Nicolaus Copernicus proposed that the planets revolved around the sun rather than the other way around, his peers promptly ridiculed and ostracized him. Yet his theory eventually proved correct.

Changing deeply imbedded beliefs is hard for most people, even us, and while we don't imagine ourselves to be anywhere near the stature of Copernicus, by writing *The New I Do*, we are asking you to rethink what you know about marriage. We acknowledge that it might feel a bit like heresy to suggest it. Since you have gotten to this point in the book, you have seen that many others have attempted to change marriage, too—from anthropologist Margaret Mead, who championed trial marriages, to Ben B. Lindsey, who lost his judgeship when he suggested young adults could have a "companionate marriage," from the progressives who dabbled in alternative marriages in their quest to make monogamy voluntary instead of compulsory, to Ryan and Lisa, who married not with a promise to be together forever, but just until they had done what they set out to do—have a child together and commit to being the best co-parents they can be for eighteen years.

Maybe that all sounds blasphemous to you, but, when you look at how people are already choosing to structure their romantic relationships, we think it's smart to question why society continues to hold onto one model of marriage when the people have already spoken—they just will not be bound by those rules anymore. While arrangements like Ryan and Lisa's may seem unusual, they actually have a lot in common with the "traditional" reason to get married—to bring children into the world in a supportive, loving, and stable environment. Their purpose-driven coming together is one of the most rational and grounded reasons we have ever heard of for two people to tie the knot, and trust us—we have been to *a lot* of weddings.

Your marriage license, or the one you plan to get one day, doesn't require you to *do* anything or *be* anything either. It just is a legal document that says, yes, you're married, and because of that, you and your beloved are entitled to a lot of government perks (while also finally being relieved of ever having to hear your Aunt Ethel ask, "So, when are you finally going to get married?"). While busybody aunts will always feel entitled to ask you about your love life (they most likely baby-sat you, burped you, and changed your diapers, so it might be payback time), many wonder why the government needs to know about it.

Why indeed. Why should the state have any say in your romantic partnership? Why should the government give benefits to you because you got hitched and others haven't—even if they tried really hard to make it happen? Why should the state decide that some relationships are "worthy" and valuable and others aren't? How does the state even know that a couple is entering into a union with the best possible intentions and therefore deserves all those perks? And why should the government care? Since people are already successfully fashioning all sorts of consensual and committed relationships that embrace a multitude of ways to live, love, and caregive, it appears that they are fully capable of defining their own marital rules and how they might want to dissolve their marriage. Why can't two people make their own decisions about how to be in a relationship? And why should those arrangements miss out on government benefits just because they may not be based on romantic love?

Many of us are pondering these questions lately. What about you? Do you really care if the state validates your marriage license? Would you still have the same love, devotion, respect, and commitment to your spouse or potential spouse if your marriage weren't sanctioned by the state? Would you still want to be with your sweetie if the government didn't offer you financial incentives to be together?

While state laws define who may marry and what happens when a marriage ends, whether by divorce or death, the laws have little say about what occurs within a marriage. Spouses truly are on their own when it comes to their day-to-day interactions, the way they define their roles and share responsibilities, and how they behave toward each other and their children (except, obviously, in instances of domestic violence, marital rape, or child abuse or neglect).

DO WE REALLY NEED MARRIAGE?

Some scholars and academics argue that marriage should no longer have legal status, thereby removing the state from all things marital. That doesn't mean marriage would necessarily go away; the uniting of two people still has incredible symbolic significance, as this book has illustrated. Instead, marriage might continue as a social, cultural, or religious institution, or some combination of the three. But government would no longer have a say in it.

Despite the various forms of family nowadays and despite the high divorce rate, many believe that the relative stability, commitment, and mutual dependency marriage creates is still the best environment for raising kids, and many people marry because they wish to raise a family. Laws were set up to help spouses do just that. Society has an interest and a duty to protect its most vulnerable—the young, the old, the ill, and the disabled—yet current marriage laws leave a lot of other kinds of people in need of care unprotected.

What about the people who, for whatever reason, are unmarried but have children? They are unprotected. Same-sex couples have long been denied the right to marry, yet about 6 million children of all ages have parents who are LBGT. They are unprotected. More than 5 million children live in a household headed by a grandparent. They are unprotected.

Do those children and caregivers not count? Don't they deserve legal safeguards, too? We say they do. Can society do better? We believe it can.

Emory University law professor Martha Albertson Fineman says the economic and social privileges marriage offers should instead be given to a different family form than the nuclear family—that of caretaker and dependent. Society has historically relied on married couples to "manage dependency," she writes, both of children and unemployed wives who stayed home and cared for the children. But women have more economic freedom nowadays and don't need marriage to protect them, as we discussed in previous chapters. Expectations and desires for marriage today are far removed from what couples expected and wanted years ago. Instead of promoting marriage, many say the state should be doing its best to encourage and support responsible, stable, and committed caregiving, no matter what form it takes.

"The most compelling reason to end legal interest in marital status is the simple ethical obligation to treat the wide variety of caretaking relationships fairly," write Dorian Solot and Marshall Miller, founders of Alternatives to Marriage Project, now called Unmarried Equality.

Among the ideas being proposed are state-recognized Intimate Care-Giving Union (ICGU) statutes, which recognize that those who caregive are often economically vulnerable and offer protections to reduce their risks. Others suggest the idea of a "minimal marriage," which also acknowledges and protects caregiving relationships and sets up some legal restrictions on who can have marital rights. It doesn't, however, require that those rights be exchanged with just one person, since adults have all sorts of caring relationships with a variety of people—whether nonexclusive sexual relationships as practiced by polyamorists; or those offering financial or emotional support, such as adult children who look after an aging parent or a friend; or people who share a household and finances but not necessarily sex. Others suggest expanding traditional nuclear families to become "combination families" or "combos"—three to eight adult members who gather for the purpose of co-parenting and sharing domestic and economic responsibilities, whether in one household or several nearby (sounding somewhat like a more modern take on the communes of the 1960s and '70s). Like so many of the models presented in this book, those sorts of "combo" arrangements already exist to various degrees.

Still others suggest a pluralistic model of marriage. Instead of directing people toward one social institution, traditional marriage, the state would help create numerous institutions with various "package deals" of benefits that would give couples the freedom to choose the model that works best for them, similar to the three levels of marriage the Greeks and Romans had. Again, that's already happening—Covenant Marriages, as you've seen in a previous chapter, while not widespread, are an alternative model to traditional marriage. Why not offer other models as well?

At the heart of each of these proposals is the idea that society should be more equitable while also protecting its most vulnerable. By extending benefits to those who caregive, the definition of family would be broadened to reflect all the nontraditional families that already exist and ones that may develop in the future. Single parents would get the support they need, as would whoever cares for the elderly, disabled, or sick—from childfree couples to singletons. Children would benefit greatly, whether they have one, two, or multiple parents; whether they have gay or straight parents; or whether they are being raised by grandparents or other relatives, friends, or caregivers. In other words, society as a whole would be much better served if it created safety nets that have nothing to do with partnerships based on love, gender, intimacy, and dependency.

Although we only addressed changing marriage in these pages, it's clear that there is lots of room for growth and transformation when it comes to family. We believe strongly that, if marriage as it is doesn't evolve, the downward trend of partakers will continue—even with the added gay and lesbian populations increasing the numbers. Our current version of marriage keeps us stuck in the status quo, and it shames people regardless of which side of the vows they are on.

"A society without marriage is one with no divorce and with no spinsters or bachelors, widows or widowers, or unmarried solitary individuals of any sort," author and sociologist Judith Stacey notes. "Nobody's social status or fate hinges on the success or failure of their love life or marriage."

So what's our incentive to keep this outdated model? Rather than do away with state-sanctioned marriage, law professor Martha M. Ertman proposes that business models be extended to intimate relationships through domestic relations law. "An understanding of marriage as akin to corporations, cohabitation as akin to partner-ships, and polyamory as akin to limited liability companies would enable us to avoid attaching moral judgments to the differences among those relationships. Regulation would turn on the functional needs of particular arrangements rather than moralistic reasoning and ideas about naturalistic hierarchy."

It also would alleviate inequalities, not only within relation-ships (such as between the homemaker and the breadwinner), but also among the many flavors of relationships people have today. And, it would provide a safety net for those who don't have rights and pro-tections under current laws, such as couples that cohabit.

While it won't solve every problem, Ertman believes it offers "the unique promise of providing new ways of understanding basic financial issues that family law, hampered by outdated notions of status, has failed to resolve."

IT'S TIME TO QUESTION OUR ASSUMPTIONS

Whether you agree with these kinds of radical reinventions of part-nerships or not, it's clear that many have begun to question the assumptions society has about intimate relationships, marriage, and family. We don't see a downside to that; in fact, we believe that examining what society has accepted—and often insisted—as "the norm" is a step forward. We believe it should move from being a private conversation between a couple contemplating how they want to spend time together in a committed relationship and for what purpose to a broader, open, and honest societal discussion about coupling.

Marriage has already shifted from an institutional model, in which husbands ruled the roost and there was a clear division of gendered labor, to a companionate model, in which love, friendship, and partnership are emphasized, to an individualistic model, in which personal choice, happiness, and self-development determine whether a marriage is successful or not. Family law has slowly morphed to address those shifts, including the adoption of no-fault divorce.

If nothing else, the dramatic changes in the marital landscape over the decades has proven that marriage can be an incredibly adaptable and inclusive institution—if it's called on to be so.

Early in this book, we proposed an Occupy Marriage movement because we believe that marriage will work better and be more successful if people like you start taking ownership of it. That means you will have to think consciously about what you want to get from your marriage.

If you are already married and believe that you have played out your current marital model for all it is worth (a traditional marriage, we presume), why not reinvent and reinvigorate it—not by "working harder" at it, as so-called "experts" will advise, but by starting from scratch with a new way of experiencing it. Consider it a new job description; you used to be in charge of making sure X happened. Now, you are responsible for the success of Y and Z. It's a new challenge that requires you to be innovative, open-minded, and flexible to make sure it works. Enthusiasm helps.

We are encouraged that more men and women are increasingly accepting the idea of nontraditional families—same-sex marriage, unmarried couples with children, and poly-families among them—and favor egalitarian marriages in which paid work, housework, and childcare duties are shared. We are encouraged that people increasingly question whether tying the knot is something they really want to do or whether they feel pressured into it. Even with the changes we lay out, marriage may not be right for everyone, and that's okay. The goal isn't to get everyone to marry, but rather to help those who choose to marry have successful unions by their definition of success. That's why we wrote this book. And we are especially encouraged that many more people—like you—are interested in exploring ways to do that.

Whether you are marrying to become parents or for companionship, whether you are hoping to improve your longtime marriage or deciding to live apart, you now know from the stories we have shared with you that these models work. The couples we interviewed have the marriages they want because they married or tweaked their partnerships with intention. That is what we consider a happy, successful marriage.

And now it's your turn to figure out what you consider a happy, successful marriage, even—and especially—if it goes against the one-size-fits-all model. This is *your* marriage, no one else's. You can make it happen.

We'll be behind you, rooting you on.

NOTES

Chapter 1

Today, "it is possible to live, love, form a family . . . " Ruspini, Elisabetta, *Diversity In Family Life: Gender, Relationships And Social Change*, University of Chicago Press, 2013.

Chapter 2

According to Gauvain, Gauvain, Jennifer, "Why So Many Of Us Marry The Wrong Person," *Huffington Post*, Sept. 21, 2011.

The vast majority, Pew Research Center, "Love Trumps Money," Jan. 6, 2011.

And couples that feel that way, Perel, Ester, "The Paradox in Passion," *Huffington Post*, Oct. 4, 2013.

In fact, one study found that, Campbell, Kelly and Wright, David W., "Marriage today: Exploring the incongruence between Americans' beliefs and practices," *Journal of Comparative Family Studies*, pages 329–345, 2010.

Having realistic expectations, McNutly, James, "Positive expectations in the early years of marriage: should couples expect the best or brace for the worst?" *Journal of Personality and Social Psychology*, pages 729–43, May 2004.

Whether or not you want to be, Adamopoulou, Effrosyni, "Peer Effects in Young Adults' Marital Decisions," *Universidad Carlos III Madrid, working paper*, October 2012.

It's what sociologist Andrew Cherlin, Cherlin, Andrew J., "In the Season of Marriage, a Question. Why Bother?" *The New York Times*, April 27, 2013.

Marriage makes people happy, Musick, Kelly and Bumpass, Larry, "Reexamining the Case for Marriage: Union Formation and Changes in Well-being," *Journal of Marriage and Family*, pages 1–18, 2012.

Married couples tend to create, Satran, Richard, "Marriage Benefit: Couples' Money Secrets Everyone Can Use," *US News*, Sept. 20, 2013.

People who are married, Siegler, Ilene C., Brummett, Beverly et al, "Consistency and Timing of Marital Transitions and Survival During Midlife: the Role of Personality and Health Risk Behaviors," *Annals of Behavioral Medicine*, 2013.

Marriage makes us healthier, Averett, Susan L., Sikora, Asia and Argys, Laura M., "For better or worse: Relationship status and body mass index," *Economics & Human Biology*, pages 330–349, December 2008; "Unhappy Marriage: Bad for Your Health," *WebMD Health News*, Dec. 5, 2005.

Married men had a 46 percent, Eaker, ED, "Marital status, marital strain, and risk of coronary heart disease or total mortality: the Framingham Offspring Study," *Psychosomatic Medicine*, pages 509–13, July 18, 2007.

Married people tend to have lower, Simon, Robin W., "The Relationship Between Marriage and Mental Health," *Psychiatry Weekly,* July 23, 2012; Denney, Justin T., "Adult Suicide Mortality in the United States: Marital Status, Family Size, Socioeconomic Status, and Differences by Sex" *Social Science Quarterly,* pages 1167–85, 2009.

Married people are less likely to smoke, Centers for Disease Control and Prevention, "Marital Status and Health: United States, 1999–2002," Advance Data, Number 351, available at http://www.cdc.gov/nchs/pressroom/04facts/marriedadults. htm.

Kids tend to do better with two, Crawford, Claire; Goodman, Alissa; Greaves, Ellen, "Cohabitation, marriage, relationships stability and child outcomes: final report," *Institute for Fiscal Studies, IFS Report R87,* October 2013.

Married people commit, Craig, Jessica; Diamond, Brie; Piquero, Alex R. "Marriage as an Intervention in the Lives of Criminal Offenders," *Effective Interventions in the Lives of Criminal Offenders,* 2014.

Some research indicates marriage, Gerstel, Naomi and Natalia Sarkisian, "Marriage: The Good, the Bad, and the Greedy," *Contexts,* pages 16–21, November 2006; Sarkisian, Natalia and Gerstel, Naomi, "Till Marriage Do Us Part: Adult Children's Relationships with Parents," *Journal of Marriage and Family,* pages 360–376, May 2008.

Interestingly, couples that live together, Musick, Kelly and Bumpass, Larry "Reexamining the Case for Marriage: Union Formation and Changes in Well-being," *Journal of Marriage and Family,* pages 1–18, February 2012.

Daughters-in-law have a lot of power, Merrill, Deborah, "Mothering Adult Sons versus Daughters: The Role of the Spouse," *Mothers of Adult Children,* pages 63–73, 2013.

Marriage may indeed be, Sarkisian, Natalia and Naomi Gerstel, "Till Marriage Do Us Part: Adult Children's Relationships with Parents," *Journal of Marriage and Family,* pages 360–376, May 2008.

You'll be happier and more committed, Aron, Arthur and Aron, Elaine N., "Self-expansion motivation and including other in the self," *Handbook of personal relationships: Theory, research, and interventions,* Second edition, pages 251–270, 1997; Lewandowski, Gary W., Jr. and Ackerman, Robert A. "Something's missing: Need fulfillment and self-expansion as predictors of susceptibility to infidelity," *The Journal of Social Psychology,* pages 389–403, 2006; Lewandowski, Gary W., Jr., Aron, Arthur et al, "Losing a self-expanding relationship: Implications for the self-concept," *Personal Relationships,* pages 317–331, 2006.

Men and women seem to be pretty, Pew Research Center, "The Decline of Marriage and Rise of New Families," November 2010.

What she concluded, and which, Loscocco, Karyn and Walzer, Susan "Gender and the Culture of Heterosexual Marriage in the United States," *Journal of Family Theory & Review,* pages 1–14, 2013.

Not only that, but wives still, "Chore wars: Men, women and housework," *National Science Foundation Discoveries,* 2008.

Poet Jill Bialosky knowingly, Bialosky, Jill, "How We Became Strangers," *The Bitch In The House: 26 Women Tell the Truth About Sex, Solitude, Work, Motherhood,* page 119, 2002.

Having to conform to societal, Pew Research Center, "The Decline of Marriage and Rise of New Families," November 2010.

Like love, it isn't, Carter, Julia, "What is commitment? Women's accounts of intimate attachment," *Families, Relationships and Societies,* pages 137–153, 2012; Wolpert, Stuart, "Here is what real commitment to your marriage means," *UCLA newsroom,* February 2012.

Some believe other things, Athill, Diana, *Somewhere Towards the End: A Memoir,* W. W. Norton & Company, 2008.

Many believe it is, but, Carter, Julia, "What is commitment? Women's accounts of intimate attachment," *Families, Relationships and Societies,* pages 137–153, 2012.

Sacrificing when life expectancy, Kinsella, Kevin G., "Changes in Life Expectancy 1900–1990," *American Journal of Clinical Nutrition,* page 55, 1992.

Each state's laws on marriage, Newton, Erik W., "You Already Have a Prenup," *New York Times Room for Debate,* March 21, 2013.

That's why the prenup, "DETAILS Of Jay Z And Beyonce's PRE-NUP . . . If They DIVORCE, Beyonce Gets $5M Per Child, Private Jet Plus MORE," *MediaTakeOut. com,* May 2, 2008.

"I would encourage any woman, "Beyonce Admits To 'Marriage Contract' With Jay," *HelloBeautiful.com,* March 15, 2010.

Prenups have been created, "Strange Prenuptial Agreements," *Divorce360.com.*

We agree with David Allen Green, Green, David Allen, "Making marriage harder," *New Statesman,* Feb. 14, 2011.

Or, as history professor Glenda, Schupack, Deborah, "'Starter' Marriages: So Early, So Brief," *The New York Times,* July 7, 1994.

Perhaps it's because they, Essig, Laurie and Owens, Lynn, "What if Marriage Is Bad for Us?" *The Chronicle of Higher Education,* Oct. 9, 2009.

Chapter 3

They've been around for, Schupack, Deborah, "'Starter' Marriages: So Early, So Brief," *The New York Times,* July 7, 1994.

Let's step back first, Rampell, Paul, "A high divorce rate means it's time to try 'wed-leases,'" *Washington Post,* Aug. 4, 2013.

Okay, those are pretty unlikely, Dew, Jeffrey, Britt, Sonya, and Huston, Sandra, "Examining the Relationship Between Financial Issues and Divorce," *Family Relations,* pages 615–628, 2012.

It's called divorce, Kreider, Rose M. and Ellis, Renee, "Number, Timing, and Duration of Marriages and Divorces: 2009," *US Census Current Population Reports,* May 2011.

Very few people, Campbell, Kelly; Wright, David W., and Floresa, Carlos G., "Newlywed women's Marital Expectations: Lifelong Monogamy?" *Journal of Divorce & Remarriage,* pages 108–125, 2012.

That doesn't mean that people, Carter, Julia, "What is commitment? Women's accounts of intimate attachment," *Families, Relationships and Societies,* pages 137–153, 2012.

Marriage contracts of, Ellis, Havelock, *Studies in the Psychology of Sex,* Wildside Press, April 30, 2008.

He was promptly booted, Simmons, Christina, *Making Marriage Modern: Women's*

Sexuality from the Progressive Era to World War II," Oxford University Press, page 1220, April 10, 2009.

It didn't pass, but, The Lena Lee Collections, Thurgood Marshall Law Library, University of Maryland Francis King Carey School of Law, available at http://www.law.umaryland.edu/marshall/specialcollections/lenaleepapers.

In 2010, a women's group, "'Renewable marriage' proposed," *abc-cbnNEWS.com*, Jan. 11, 2010.

Not every couple wants, Rasmusen, Eric B. and Stake, Jeffrey, "Lifting the Veil of Ignorance: Personalizing the Marriage Contract," *Indiana Law Journal*, pages 454–502, spring 1998.

Some people suggest that, Becker, Gary S., "Why Every Married Couple Should Sign a Contract," *Business Week*, page 30, Dec. 29, 1997.

There are about 15.3 million, "Household and Families: 2010," *Census Briefs 2010*, April 2012.

First of all, you don't, "Living Together: Legal & Financial F.A.Q.," *Unmarried Equality.*

Couples often have different expectations, Pew Research Center, "*The Decline of Marriage and Rise of New Families*," November 2010.

There's no way to easily define, Solomon, Sondra E.; Rothblum, Esther D., and Kimberly F. Balsam, "Money, Housework, Sex, and Conflict: Same-Sex Couples in Civil Unions, Those Not in Civil Unions, and Heterosexual Married Siblings," *Sex Roles*, May 2005.

In fact, cohabiting, Smock, Pamela, "Cohabitation in the United States: An Appraisal of Research Themes, Findings, and Implications," *Annual Reviews Sociology*, pages 1–20, 2000; Pew Research Center, "Modern Parenthood," March 14, 2013.

Men don't "have" to, Musick, Kelly and Bumpass, Larry, "Reexamining the Case for Marriage: Union Formation and Changes in Well-being," *Journal of Marriage and Family*, pages 1–18, 2012; Heimdal, Kristen R. and Houseknecht, Sharon K., "Cohabiting and married couples' income organization: Approaches in Sweden and the United States," *Journal of Marriage and Family*, pages 525–538, 2003.

Unlike cohabitation, Copen, Casey E., Daniels, Kimberly, and Mosher, William D., "First Premarital Cohabitation in the United States: 2006–2010," *National Health Statistics Reports No. 64*, April 4, 2013.

For the most part, Widiss, Deborah A., "Changing The Marriage Equation," *Washington University Law Review*, 2012.

What you don't want to do, Stanley, Scott M.; Rhoades, Galena K., Markman, Howard J., "Sliding vs. deciding: Inertia and the premarital cohabitation effect," *Family Relations*, pages 499–509, 2006.

"Those coming out, Peterson, Karen S., "Starter marriage: A new term for early divorce," *USA Today*, Jan. 29, 2002.

"On the surface, Klosowski, Thorin, "Relationship Advice I Wish I'd Heard Before Getting Divorced," *Lifehacker*, April 25, 2013.

"Many couples are living together, Jayson, Sharon, "When the honeymoon's over, which couples survive and why?" *USA Today*, March 5, 2012.

Chapter 4

That differs somewhat from, Pew Research Center, "Love and Marriage," Feb. 13, 2013.

The least successful stepfamilies, Bray, James H. and Kelly, John, *Stepfamilies,* Broadway Books, 1999.

The author of, Arnoldy, Ben, "America becomes a more 'adult-centered' nation," *The Christian Science Monitor,* July 10, 2007.

Marriage was what, Blackstone, Amy, "Doing Family Without Having Kids," *Sociology Compass,* pages 52–62, 2014.

We weren't sure, "Why We Get Married (Episode No. 46 with Jenna McCarthy)," *Married With Baggage,* available at http://www.marriedwithluggage.com/why-get-married-jenna-mccarthy.

Chapter 5

The studies have all looked at married, Johnson, Eric M., "Raising Darwin's Consciousness: Sarah Blaffer Hrdy on the Evolutionary Lessons of Motherhood," *Scientific American,* March 16, 2012.

Only a small percentage, Angier, Natalie, "The Changing American Family," *The New York Times,* Nov. 25, 2013.

If, as she says, some gay, Stacey, Judith, *Unhitched: Love, Marriage, and Family Values From West Hollywood to Western China,* NYU Press, May 2011, page 52.

She says that she's seeking Ellin, Abby, "Making a Child, Minus the Couple," *The New York Times,* Feb, 8, 2013.

It's not everyone's experience, Lisitsa, Ellie, "Bringing Baby Home: The Research," *The Gottman Institute Relationship Blog,* July 24, 2013.

A lucky son or daughter, Colón, Ashley, A.R. and Colón, P.A., *A History of Children: A Socio-cultural Survey Across Millennia,* Greenwood Press, 2001, page 91.

Some of these children were, Bronson, Po and Merryman, Ashley, "The Fact Book: Eye-opening Memos on Everything Family," available at http://www.pobronson.com/factbook/pages/204.html.

In the Middle Ages, some parents, Bronson, Po and Merryman, Ashley, "The Fact Book: Eye-opening Memos on Everything Family," available at http://www.pobronson.com/factbook/pages/204.html.

In one year in 1900s New York, Bronson, Po and Merryman, Ashley, "The Fact Book: Eye-opening Memos on Everything Family," available at http://www.pobronson.com/factbook/pages/204.html.

Still, millions of children are abused, Healy, Michelle, "Child neglect accounts for 75% of reported abuse cases," *USA Today,* Sept. 12, 2013; "*Fourth National Incidence Study of Child Abuse* (NIS-4), Report to Congress, 2010, available at http://www.acf.hhs.gov/sites/default/files/opre/nis4_report_congress_full_pdf_jan2010.pdf.

In fact, children who grow up in families, Tyree, Jenny, "30 Years of Research that Tell Us, 'A Child Deserves a Mother and a Father,'" *CitizenLink,* June 17, 2010.

Studies appear to confirm, Daly, Martin and Wilson, Margo, "The 'Cinderella effect': Elevated mistreatment of stepchildren in comparison to those living with genetic parents," available from http://www.cep.ucsb.edu/buller/cinderella%20effect%20facts.pdf.

Some kids do much better, Amato, Paul R., "Research on Divorce: Continuing Trends and New Developments," *Journal of Marriage and Family*, pages 650–666, June 2010.

These are the children, Emery, Robert, *The Truth About Children and Divorce: Dealing with the Emotions So You and Your Children Can Thrive*, Plume, Jan. 31, 2006.

Still, divorce seems to have long-lasting, Ryan, Rebecca and Claessens, Amy, "Associations between family structure changes and children's behavior problems: the moderating effects of timing and marital birth," *Developmental Psychology*, pages 1219–31, July 2013.

Millennials (those born between, Pew Research Center, "Millennials, Parenthood Trumps Marriage," March 9, 2011.

Chapter 6

Familiarity breeds contempt, Dean, Jeremy, "Does Familiarity Breed Liking or Contempt?" *PsyBlog*, available at http://www.spring.org.uk/2011/09/does-familiarity-breed-liking-or-contempt.php.

More wives than husbands, Bianchi, Suzanne M., Robinson, John P., and Milkie, Melissa A., "Changing Rhythms of American Family Life," *Russell Sage Foundation*, September 2007.

Even so, both rank, Bernstein, Elizabeth, "Need Space in a Relationship? Just Don't Say It That Way," *Wall Street Journal*, June 26, 2012.

"Young people are seeing, Bolick, Kate, "Divide and Conquer: Married But Separate," *Elle*, March 5, 2012.

She rejects societal pressure, Bolick, Kate, "Divide and Conquer: Married But Separate," *Elle*, March 5, 2012.

Studies indicate that women, Bergner, Daniel, "Unexcited? There May Be a Pill for That," *The New York Times Magazine*, May 22, 2013.

Some live apart by choice, Bolick, Kate, "Divide and Conquer: Married But Separate," *Elle*, March 5, 2012.

There is nothing, Fein, David J., "Spending Time Together: Time Use Estimates for Economically Disadvantaged and Non disadvantaged Married Couples in the United States," available at http://www.acf.hhs.gov/sites/default/files/opre/spending_time_together.pdf.

Often, they have even higher, Stafford, Laura, *Maintaining-Long-Distance-Cross-Residential-Relationships-Communication*, Routledge, Nov. 5, 2004.

You may not have visuals, Boutin, Chad, "Snap judgments decide a face's character, psychologist finds," *Princeton.edu*, Aug. 22, 2006, available at http://www.princeton.edu/main/news/archive/S15/62/69K40/index.xml?section=topstories.

That still doesn't mean someone, Le, B., Korn, M. S., Crockett, E. E., and Loving, T. J., "Missing you maintains us: Missing a romantic partner, commitment, relationship maintenance, and physical infidelity," *Journal of Social and Personal Relationships*, pages 653–667, 2011.

And, like an Open Marriage, Illouz, Eva, *Why Love Hurts: A Sociological Explanation*, Polity Press, March 2012.

While those choosing a long-distance, "Long Distance Relationship Frequently Asked

Questions," *LongDistanceRelationships.net.*

Recent innovations and virtual reality, Beckman, Jamie, "The creepy future of dating," *SheKnows.com*, Dec. 23, 2013.

It doesn't matter how, Sifferlin, Alexandra, "Closeness in a Relationship: Is it Overrated?" *Time*, Feb. 14, 2013.

Many also got better, Mietzner, Sara and Li-Wen, Lin, "Would You Do It Again? Relationship Skills Gained in a Long-Distance Relationship," *College Student Journal*, page 192, March 2005.

Once the wild sex, Marazziti, Donatella, "Hormonal changes when falling in love," *Psychoneuroendocrinology*, pages 931–936, August 2004.

These various live-apart, Glotzer, Richard and Federlein, Anne C., "Miles That Bind: Commuter Marriage and Family Strengths," *Michigan Family Review*, pages 7–31, 2007.

Couples that live apart, Joel, Samantha, "Living Apart, Together: Why Some Couples are Forgoing Cohabitation," *Science of Relationships.*

If the marriage dissolves, Hirschle, Jochen, "Reorganizing social life after separation," paper presented at the European Network for the Sociological & Demographic Study of Divorce, Oxford, Oct. 26–28, 2013, available at http://cv-jh.com/Hirschle_SeparationConsequences_Oxford2013.pdf; Blow, *Adrian J.* and Hartnett, Kelley, "Infidelity in Committed Relationships II: A Substantive Review," *Journal of Marital and Family Therapy*, pages 217–233, 2005.

Chapter 7

In 1947, the divorce rate, NEA, "French Divorce Rate Worries Sociologists," *The Evening Independent*, May 25, 1950.

The measure lost with, Divorce Reform Page, "The First Covenant Marriage Proposal," *Americans for Divorce Reform*, available at http://www.divorcereform.org/maz.html.

Only two states followed, Divorce Reform Page, "Covenant Marriage Legislation," *Americans for Divorce Reform*; Allman, Kevin, "Covenant Marriage Laws in Louisiana," *Gambit*, March 2, 2009.

Many people recommend premarital, Stanley, Scott M., Amato, Paul, et al, "Premarital education, marital quality, and marital stability: Findings from a large, random household survey," *Journal of Family Psychology*, pages 117–126, March 2006.

Covenant Marriage was founded by, Nock, Steven L., Sanchez, Laura A., and Wright, James D., *Covenant Marriage: The Movement to Reclaim Tradition in America*, Rutgers University Press, pages 79–81, July 16, 2008.

While religion plays a role, Spaht, Katherine Shaw, "Louisiana's Covenant Marriage: Social Commentary And Legal Implications," available at faculty.law.lsu.edu/katherinespaht.

While they've done little to, Allman, Kevin, "Covenant Marriage Laws in Louisiana," *Gambit*, March 2, 2009.

To date, there is no information, Feig, Ellen, "Is Covenant Marriage the answer to a rising divorce rate?" *LegalZoom.com*, available at http://www.legalzoom.com/marriage-divorce-family-law/divorce/is-covenant-marriage-answer.

Covenant Marriages are associated with, Feig, Ellen, "Is Covenant Marriage the answer to a rising divorce rate?" *LegalZoom.com,* available at http://www.legalzoom.com/marriage-divorce-family-law/divorce/is-covenant-marriage-answer.

Some have criticized, Olson, Waiter, "Free to Commit," *Reason,* October 1997.

And of the couples that didn't, Weigel, Jen, "Therapy before vows? Experts say 'I do'," *Chicago Tribune,* April 7, 2011.

One study found that, Sanchez, Laura and Nock, Steven, et al "Social and Demographic Factors Associated with Couples Choice between Covenant and Standard Marriage in Louisiana," available at http://opr.princeton.edu/seminars/nock.f02.pdf.

Ironically, as we were, Gibbons, Kate, "Colorado ballot measure proposes education classes to marry," *Denver Post,* Jan. 20, 2014.

While a Covenant Marriage couple, "Research FAQs," *The Gottman Institute.*

You also must sign a modified, Louisiana for Marriage, a project of Louisiana Family Forum Action; NWA Healthy Marriages, The Center for Relationship Enrichment; "Covenant Marriage in Arizona," available at http://www.azcourts.gov/Portals/31/Other%20DR/covenant.pdf.

Covenant women become more, Nock, Steven L., Sanchez, Laura A., and Wright, James D., *Covenant Marriage: The Movement to Reclaim Tradition in America,* University Press, page 113, July 16, 2008.

Covenant women are less, Steven L. Nock, Laura Ann Sanchez, James D. Wright, *Covenant Marriage: The Movement to Reclaim Tradition in America,* University Press, page 13, July 16, 2008.

Covenant men become, Steven L. Nock, Laura Ann Sanchez, James D. Wright, *Covenant Marriage: The Movement to Reclaim Tradition in America,* University Press, page 113, July 16, 2008.

Chapter 8

Yes, there is a prenup, Watkins, Jade, "'I married him for security': Crystal Harris reveals the real reason why she married Hugh Hefner," *Daily Mail,* Feb. 7, 2013.

Many of the correspondents, CRG Staff and Carlson, Terri, "Will Marry for Health Insurance," *Council for Responsible Genetics,* 2014.

"It's kind of against the notion, "Marrying for Love . . . of Money," Frank, Robert, *Wall Street Journal The Wealth Report,* Dec. 14, 2007.

Another study by evolutionary, Buss, David M. and Shackelford, Todd K. Evolutionary Psychology, "Attractive Women Want it All: Good Genes, Economic Investment, Parenting Proclivities, and Emotional Commitment," *Evolutionary Psychology,* pages, 134–146, 2008, available at http://www.epjournal.net/wp-content/uploads/EP06134146.pdf.

The couples in which the wife, Bertrand, Marianne, Kamenica, Emir, and Pan, Jessica, "Gender identity and relative income within households," October 2013, available at http://faculty.chicagobooth.edu/emir.kamenica/documents/identity.pdf.

People without a college education, Isen, Adam and Stevenson, Betsey, "Women's Education And Family Behavior: Trends In Marriage, Divorce And Fertility," *Wharton, University of Pennsylvania,* Nov. 1, 2012.

Studies have shown that although, Cherlin, Andrew, Cross-Barnet, Caitlin, and Garrett-Peters, Raymond, "Promises They Can Keep: Low-Income Women's Attitudes Toward Motherhood, Marriage, and Divorce," *Journal of Marriage and Family*, pages 919–933, Nov. 1, 2008.

It was actually easier, Wolpert, Stuart, "Poor People Value Marriage As Much As The Middle Class And Rich, Study Shows," *University of California Los Angeles*, July 16, 2012.

Since research indicates that couples, Dew, Jeffrey, Britt, Sonya, and Huston, Sandra, "Examining the Relationship Between Financial Issues and Divorce," *Family Relations*, pages 615–628, 2012.

The important thing is, Chapman, Melissa, "Can money problems kill your marriage-hell to the yeah," *Huffington Post*, Dec. 18, 2012.

In fact, a third of American couples, Trotta, Daniel and Reaney, Patricia, "Three in 10 Americans commit financial infidelity?" *Reuters*, Jan. 13, 2011.

It experienced a huge spike, Hu, Elise, "U.S. Shutdown May Be Driving Traffic To 'Sugar Daddy' Sites," *All Tech Considered*, Oct. 5, 2013.

The GDI can prevent a future, Ford, Elizabeth, and Drake, Daniela, "Smart Girls Marry Money," *Forbes*, Aug. 18, 2010.

They also need to pay attention, Blumenthal, Karen, "Girls Just Want to Have Funds," *Wall Street Journal*, May 21, 2011.

Do you both share, Dean, Ginger, "Smart Women Marry for Money," *Consumerism Commentary*, Nov. 25, 2013.

Not everyone needs to be, Leddy, Chuck, "Money, marriage, kids," *Harvard Gazette*, Feb. 21, 2013.

Many wives—perhaps as many, Davies, Erin, "As Men's Job Losses Mount, Wives Feel the Impact," *Time*, July 8, 2009.

Joblessness and economic instability, St. George, Donna, "Recession Has More Moms Entering Workforce," *Washington Post*, Feb. 12, 2010.

Talking openly and honestly, Bortz, Daniel, "5 ways couples can end money spats," *U.S. News & World Report*, Jan. 16, 2013.

Chapter 9

Instead of seeing it as, Jackson, Stevi and Scott, Sue, "The personal is still political: Heterosexuality, feminism and monogamy," *Feminism and Psychology*, pages 151–157, 2004.

Most people believe, Pew Research Center, "Modern Marriage," July 18, 2007.

Sex, or rather the lack of it, Kerner, Ian, "Are you willing to negotiate monogamy?," *CNN Blogs The Chart*, May 19, 2011.

Let's face it, McCarthy, Ellen, "Psychologist Barry McCarthy helps couples resolve sex problems," *Washington Post*, Dec. 6, 2009.

As much as people, Pew Research Center, "Modern Marriage," July 18, 2007.

Studies indicate that infidelity, Barker, Meg and Langdridge, Darren, "Whatever happened to non-monogamies? Critical reflections on recent research and theory," *Sexualities*, pages 748–772, 2010; Atwood, Joan D. and Limor Schwartz, "Cyber-Sex

The New Affair Treatment Considerations," *Journal of Couple & Relationship Therapy: Innovations in Clinical and Educational Interventions*, pages 37–56, 2002.

Unless, of course, Bryner, Jeanna, "Are Humans Meant to Be Monogamous?" *LiveScience*, Sept. 6, 2012.

And, let's not forget, Kornbluth, Jesse, "Mating in Captivity: Esther Perel Reconciles 'Sex' and 'Marriage,'" *Huffington Post*, Oct. 30, 2007.

Like Stacey, Savage, and, Savage, Dan, *American Savage: Insights, Slights, and Fights on Faith, Sex, Love, and Politics*, Dutton Adult, page 31, May 28, 2013.

It isn't as rare, Conley, Terry D., Moors, Amy C., Matsick, Jes. L., and Ziegler, Ali, "The fewer the merrier? Assessing stigma surrounding consensual non–monogamous romantic relationships," *Analyses of Social Issues and Public Policy*, pages 1–29, 2012.

Not everyone embracing an alt, Barker, Meg and Langdridge, Darren, *Understanding Non-Monogamies*, Routledge, Dec. 8, 2009.

Some suggest that monogamy's, Jackson, Stevi and Scott, Sue, "The personal is still political: Heterosexuality, feminism and monogamy," *Feminism and Psychology*, pages 151–157, 2004.

Meanwhile, monogamy for, Bryner, Jeanna, "Are Humans Meant to Be Monogamous?" *LiveScience*, Sept. 6, 2012.

We're not suggesting that consensual, Conley, Terry D., Ziegler, et al, "A critical examination of popular assumptions about the benefits and outcomes of monogamous relationships," *Personality and Social Psychology Review*, 2012; Marianne Bauer and Marianne Pieper, "'Polyamory and Mono-normativity—Results of an Empirical Study of Non-monogamous Patterns of Intimacy," unpublished article, available at https://sites.google.com/site/iapc2013homepage/presenters/marianne-pieper-ph-d, 2006.

Not only that, but we know, Conley, Terri D.; Moors, Amy C. ; Ziegler, Ali, and Karathanasis, Constantina, "Unfaithful Individuals are Less Likely to Practice Safer Sex Than Openly Nonmonogamous Individuals," *The Journal of Sexual Medicine*, 2012; Pappas, Stephanie, "New Sexual Revolution: Polyamory May Be Good for You," *LiveScience*, Feb. 14, 2013.

Well, it's not much different, Barash, David, "The myth of monogamy," *Salon*, Jan. 23, 2001.

As sociologist Stephanie Coontz, Coontz, Stephanie, *Marriage, a History*, Viking, 2005.

A third indicated, Buss, David M., *The Dangerous Passion: Why Jealousy Is as Necessary as Love and Sex*, Free Press, Feb. 14, 2000.

"All the questions with which, Moore, Thomas, "Schooled in Jealousy," *WebMD*, Feb. 12, 2009.

Of course, not every open, Anapol, Deborah, "Polyamory and Children," *Psychology Today, Love Without Limits Blog*, March 25, 2011.

Chapter 10

It's no coincidence that, Morgan and Turner, "Marriage Success Training," *StayHitched. com*, 2001 .

The truth is, most people, Wicker, Alden, "Embarrassed to Ask About Prenups," *Learn-Vest,* #3 July 2, 2013.

As long as you both have input, Wicker, Alden, "Embarrassed to Ask About Prenups," *LearnVest,* #2 July 2, 2013.

For example, student loan debt, Wicker, Alden, "Embarrassed to Ask About Prenups," *LearnVest,* #3 & #7 July 2, 2013.

Most attorneys will tell you, Landers, Jeff, "Five Reasons Your Prenup Might Be Invalid," *Forbes,* April 2, 2013.

Even Nolo, a leading publisher, Stoner, Katherine, "Prenuptial Agreement Lawyers: Do You Need One?" *Nolo Press,* available at http://www.nolo.com/legal-encyclopedia/prenuptial-agreement-lawyers-30035.html.

Prenups establish agreements, Wicker, Alden, "Embarrassed to Ask About Prenups," *LearnVest,* #2 July 2, 2013.

Fidelity clauses are not valid, Wicker, Alden, "Embarrassed to Ask About Prenups," *LearnVest,* #2 July 2, 2013.

It's your "financial mission statement, Wicker, Alden, "Embarrassed to Ask About Prenups," *LearnVest,* #2 July 2, 2013.

The Statue of Frauds, Landers, Jeff, "Five Reasons Your Prenup Might Be Invalid," *Forbes,* April 2, 2013.

Each spouse must also act, LaMance, Ken, "Fiduciary Duty of Husband and Wife Lawyers," *LegalMatch Law Library,* June 30, 2009.

Unfortunately, a fair number, Landers, Jeff, "Five Reasons Your Prenup Might Be Invalid," *Forbes,* April 2, 2013.

Once your prenup is signed, Wicker, Alden, "Embarrassed to Ask About Prenups," *Learn-Vest,* #8 July 2, 2013.

In fact, this is often one, Wicker, Alden, "Embarrassed to Ask About Prenups," *Learn-Vest,* #6 July 2, 2013.

Even if you were to, Stoner, Katherine, "Prenuptial Agreement Lawyers: Do You Need One?" *Nolo Press,* 2014.

However, this is a complex, "What Can and Cannot be Included in Prenuptial Agreements," *Findlaw,* 2014.

As you'll learn later, Wicker, Alden, "Embarrassed to Ask About Prenups," *LearnVest,* #2 July 2, 2013 and Stoner, Katherine, "Prenuptial Agreement Lawyers: Do You Need One?" *Nolo Press,* 2014.

Prenups merely allow you, Landers, Jeff, "Five Reasons Your Prenup Might Be Invalid," *Forbes,* April 2, 2013.

Prenups merely allow you, Newton, Eric, "You Already Have a Prenup," *The New York Times,* March 21, 2013.

That said, despite the new, Wicker, Alden, "Embarrassed to Ask About Prenups," *Learn-Vest,* #6 July 2, 2013.

And since many older people, Tanaka, Sanette, "The Growing Popularity of the Prenup," *Wall Street Journal,* Oct. 31, 2013 .

Keep in mind that, Landers, Jeff, "Five Reasons Your Prenup Might Be Invalid," *Forbes,* April 2, 2013.

Presenting a prenup, Landers, Jeff, "Five Reasons Your Prenup Might Be Invalid," *Forbes,* April 2, 2013.

So rather than it being, Stoner, Katherine, "Prenuptial Agreement Lawyers: Do You Need One?" *Nolo Press,* 2014.

Chapter 11

Same-sex couples have, "Six Million American Children and Adults Have an LGBT Parent," *The Williams Institute,* Feb. 27, 2013.

"The most compelling, Solot, Dorian and Miller, Marshall, "Families Win if the State Gets Out of the Marriage Business," *Marriage Proposals: Questioning a Legal Status,* NYU Press, Dec. 1, 2008.

Among the ideas being proposed, Metz, Tamara, *Untying the Knot: Marriage, the State, and the Case for Their Divorce,* Princeton University Press, 2010.

Others suggest the idea, Brake, Elizabeth, "What Political Liberalism Implies for Marriage Law," *Ethics,* pages 302–337, January 2010.

Others suggest expanding, Anapol, Deborah T., "The Future of The Family and The Fate of Our Children," *LoveWithoutLimits.com,* available at http://www.lovewithoutlimits.com/articles/The_Future_of_The_Family.html.

Still others suggest a pluralistic, Lifshitz, Shahar, "The Pluralistic Vision of Marriage," *Marriage At Crossroads,* Cambridge Publishing, 2012.

While it won't solve every problem, Ertman, Martha M., "The Business of Intimacy," *Feminism Confronts Homo Economicus: Gender, Law, and Society,* Cornell University Press, 2005.

We are encouraged that more men, Pew Research Center, "For young adults, the ideal marriage meets reality," July 10, 2013.

ABOUT THE AUTHORS

Susan Pease Gadoua, LCSW, is an author and therapist who lives in Sonoma County, California, with her husband and dogs. She is the founder and executive director of Changing Marriage, an agency that provides innovative approaches to marriage designed to set people up to succeed from beginning to end. This work is done through her support groups, couples' therapy sessions as well as in the many classes (online and in person) and retreats she offers. Susan is available for individual consultations as well.

Susan's previous books include *San Francisco Chronicle* best-seller *Contemplating Divorce, a Step-by-Step Guide to Deciding Whether to Stay or Go* and *Stronger Day by Day, Reflections for Healing and Rebuilding After Divorce*. She is also the author of the e-book *The Top Ten Misguided Reasons to Stay in a Bad Marriage*.

She has appeared on television, radio and in print, including The CBS Early Show and publications such as *The Wall Street Journal, USA Today, The Washington Post*, and *Psychology Today*. Susan writes regular columns for The Huffington Post and PsychologyToday.com.

For more information on Susan, visit her website at www.changingmarriage.com or email her at info@changingmarriage.com. You can also follow Susan on her social media outlets that include her LinkedIn Changing Marriage Group, her Changing Marriage Page on Facebook and on Twitter @changingmarriag.

Vicki Larson is a longtime award-winning journalist, freelancer, blogger, and columnist. She has been a featured blogger for The Huffington Post; columnist for Mommy Tracked: Managing the Chaos of Modern Motherhood, ModernMom.com, and Divorce360; and contributor to the anthologies *Nothing But the Truth So Help Me God: 73 Women on Life's Transitions* and *Knowing Pains: Women on Love, Sex and Work in Our 40s*. She has appeared on television, radio, and print, including the *New York Times* Room for Debate, MPR's "The Daily Circuit," and Australia's "The Daily Edition." She is the mother of two young men, and she lives in the San Francisco Bay Area. Follow her blog, OMG Chronicles, and find her on Facebook at www.facebook.com/vlarson, LinkedIn at www.linkedin.com/in/vickilarson, and Twitter @OMGchronicles.

CPSIA information can be obtained
at www.ICGtesting.com
Printed in the USA
LVOW07s0538290717
543070LV00001B/94/P